# IT'S YOUR WEDDING

T0383492

# IT'S YOUR WEDDING

## A Step by Step Guide
## Down the Aisle

## GEORGIE MITCHELL

Michael O'Mara Books Limited

For Isla, the exclamation mark in the happiest sentence I will ever write.

First published in Great Britain in 2025 by
Michael O'Mara Books Limited
9 Lion Yard, Tremadoc Road, London SW4 7NQ

A CIP catalogue record for this book is available from the British Library.

Papers used by Michael O'Mara Books Limited are natural, recyclable products made from wood grown in sustainable forests. The manufacturing processes conform to the environmental regulations of the country of origin.

ISBN: 978-1-78929-689-1 in paperback print format

1 2 3 4 5 6 7 8 9 10

www.mombooks.com

Cover designed by Anna Morrison
Illustrations and design by Jade Wheaton

Printed and bound in China

MIX
Paper | Supporting responsible forestry
FSC
www.fsc.org    FSC® C010256

# CONTENTS

# FOREWORD

From Georgie's famous BLOW ME tip, we've been hooked. What she doesn't know about weddings isn't worth knowing, and now, finally, all her wisdom is wrapped up in one delightful package.

Your wedding day is one of the most significant days of your life, yet often there's little guidance on whether what you're doing is right – until now. Consider this book your ultimate wedding planning bible. It contains everything you need to know to ensure your wedding day runs smoothly and, most importantly, represents you both!

What's a shot list? Who needs reserved signs? What time should your ceremony start? All your questions are answered here, with a sprinkle of humour to keep you smiling through the planning process.

Georgie's expertise is your secret weapon, ensuring your wedding is as beautiful and seamless as you've always dreamed. So relax, dive in, and let this guide transform your wedding planning journey into a fun and informed process.

Here's to making your wedding as personal, fun and epic as you are – with a few laughs along the way!

**Jamie Laing**

# INTRODUCTION

Trends arrive and disappear, friends' and families' opinions will be forgotten, arguments will be in the past and your wedding day will come and go. So do it your way. Embrace your individualism, enjoy your quirks, go against the grain, challenge the traditions and enjoy yourselves. You only get to do this wedding once!

Hi, I'm Georgie, wedding planner and coordinator – and bride of 2022. My intention for this book is to fill you with ideas, knowledge and inspiration for your wedding. I'm here to give you the information you need to make your wedding truly spectacular, unique and one of the best days of your life.

During the planning, you will swing between fun and frustration. That's normal! Trust the process and keep an eye on the bigger picture – you get to marry your person ... That said, if you *are* going to marry your person, do it bloody well.

This book is filled with the best ways to make sure your day runs seamlessly. Tips on how to add little moments you'll remember forever and ways to use those personal touches. Take the bits that are good for you and ignore the parts that you don't enjoy. It's on the cover, but I'll tell you again: it's *your* wedding day.

**Georgie Mitchell**

# CHAPTER 1

# Congratulations

# The engagement balloons have deflated, now what?

Congratulations! I'm hoping you are absolutely bursting with joy right now – and my first tip is to remember this feeling. Wedding planning will get hard, people are going to piss you off and you may debate just sacking it all off and eloping to the Caribbean, but that's all normal, so power through. The very first thing you're going to do as a couple is arrange a date to sit down and talk. No, it's not a counselling session, but you are going to work through these questions:

What is the most important part of the wedding to us?

Who do we need there?

What budget are we able to spend?

What are we both known for?

What budget are we comfortable with spending?

What do we both care about most?

Who do we want there?

What are we expecting from our big day?

## What is the most important part of the wedding to us?

This is not a trick question, so you can't be annoyed at each other. It's also OK for you to have different answers. Discuss what element you care most about. Is it the food, drink, entertainment, everyone being together, a big party? This will help you figure out where your budget is best spent and make it *your* wedding.

## What budget are we able to spend?

Are you paying for it all? How much can you save each month? Are you using a credit card? Do you have any savings? Are any parents or family supporting financially? It's going to be an awkward conversation, but explain to family that you're starting to plan your wedding; ask whether they would like to contribute and, if so, by how much or what element they would like to contribute towards.

## What budget are we comfortable with spending?

This is a very different question to the one above. What you can spend and what you *want* to spend are not the same thing. There is a very fine line between this being the biggest day of your life and still just one day. You need to wake up the next day and feel like every penny was very well spent. This could be wedding-planning argument number one (I say this with experience), so it's important to work through the discussion and compromise.

## Who do we want there?

This is the easy list: family, friends, co-workers, anyone who you like and want to be there.

## Who do we need there?

I know this sucks, but there are probably people you *have* to have at your wedding, whether that's partners of important people, family members, mothers-in-law ... Combining this list with the one above should give you your guest list. And you need to have your guest list before you start venue hunting. There's no point looking at venues that can only hold fifty guests if your must-have list way exceeds sixty!

## What are we both known for?

This might seem like an odd question, but it's important to be true to yourselves when you're thinking about your wedding. What are your guests expecting from you? Are you the party people and therefore a band would be a no-brainer? Are you into your wines and cocktails and therefore a free bar is non-negotiable? Are you full of humour and a traditional ceremony would be weird? These are all things you need to know now, especially before booking a venue, to ensure you can do everything you want to do.

## What do we both care about most?

Work your way through these and mark how important they are to you both, with 1 being not important and 10 being essential!

| | |
|---|---|
| Licensed ceremony space | 1 2 3 4 5 6 7 8 9 10 |
| Accommodation onsite | 1 2 3 4 5 6 7 8 9 10 |
| Close to home | 1 2 3 4 5 6 7 8 9 10 |
| Allow bands | 1 2 3 4 5 6 7 8 9 10 |
| Allow outside catering | 1 2 3 4 5 6 7 8 9 10 |
| Multi-day hire | 1 2 3 4 5 6 7 8 9 10 |
| Good inside spaces | 1 2 3 4 5 6 7 8 9 10 |
| Weekend availability | 1 2 3 4 5 6 7 8 9 10 |
| Exclusive use | 1 2 3 4 5 6 7 8 9 10 |
| Easy accessibility | 1 2 3 4 5 6 7 8 9 10 |
| Nice grounds | 1 2 3 4 5 6 7 8 9 10 |

Use this as your guide and a reminder of the details that are important to you. Try not to let social media, suppliers or loved ones sway you from this.

## What are we expecting from our big day?

Don't give me the love-and-marriage crap – what do you really want? There's no shade in saying you want to get drunk, have Instagrammable decor or show off to your mates that you know how to plan an epic party. The more honest you can be at this point, the better. It'll mean you can allocate your budget more effectively. It'll also give you a starting point when you think about venues and suppliers.

Another thing to consider is how much work you're expecting to do. An article from MarthaStewart.com stated that couples will spend between 200 and 300 hours planning their wedding. If you immediately think that's not for you, then maybe the first thing to do is consult a wedding planner.

Finally, who's planning what? Now, don't cancel me for saying this, but *typically* there's one person who isn't as involved as the other ... I'll let you guess who. But what parts do they want to be involved in? Is music their jam? Does food really get their juices flowing? Is the budget all they care about?

Equally, how much involvement do you want from them? Do you both need to agree to a monthly wedding check-in? Do you want to be left alone? Just take this point in the book as a reminder to have the conversation. It's easier to lay out the ground rules and expectations before it all gets stressful.

# THE RINGS

Before we start planning the big day, let's talk about the engagement ring. *Hopefully* you've got a ring that is perfect for you, whether that's a new shiny piece or a family heirloom that you love. Let me give you the lowdown on the next steps ...

## Book or get started on your first 'bridal mani'

Everyone is going to be looking at your hands. Whether they're looking at a perfectly captured Instagram snap or seeing you in person, all eyes will be on your engagement ring and, in turn, your hands. And nobody will notice your lovely ring if your chipped nails are ruining the vibe.

## Your engagement ring doesn't fit

If your ring doesn't fit, don't stress – but do take it off! If the ring is too big you're going to damage or lose it, and if it's too small you're going to damage your finger. I know you don't want to take it off, but a moment of sorrow is worth a lifetime of the perfect fit. Contact the jeweller that made your ring and discuss having it resized. Be very cautious about having your ring resized by a different company. Check your manufacturer's terms and conditions, as this may void your warranty!

## Get to know your ring

You need to know your ring. Learn what the cut, gem and metal type are so you can properly care for it. For example, if your ring is an opal, you cannot get it wet (not even in hand washing!), while emerald rings can't go in ultrasonic cleaners. And so on ... Knowing your ring will save you time and money in the long run. Don't be afraid to reach out to the jeweller that made it and ask for a little what's what.

## Insure your ring

The next step is to get that ring insured. Stop reading this book right now and sort it out. Most home insurance companies will cover you for loss, theft and damage, but you need to check!

## Store your paperwork safely

Most engagement rings come with a lot of paperwork. While the receipt may be top secret from you, do be sure to have the valuation provided by your jeweller stored in a safe place at home, along with any diamond certification, your warranty and other relevant information.

## How to look after your ring

These are the golden rules you should be living by:

1. Remove your ring before any strenuous or manual activities.
2. Remove your ring before showering and putting on skincare, makeup and perfume.
3. Keep your rings away from chemicals.
4. Don't wear your ring while sleeping.

## Comparison is the thief of joy

Your engagement ring symbolizes the start of the rest of your lives together, so don't begin by comparing notes about quality, size and price with your friends and family members. All that matters is that your partner was thinking of you and your preferences when choosing it and that you love your ring and what it stands for.

## You hate the ring

This is awkward, but honesty is the best policy. While I don't recommend telling your partner straight away, it is something you'll need to say. You will be wearing that ring for the rest of your life, and it's important for it to be right. It's likely that you can make changes to your current ring, like using the stones in a different setting. Alternatively, you might be able to enhance your engagement ring by choosing a wedding band that adds a bit of spice.

## How to find wedding bands

Do not leave getting your wedding bands till the last minute – this is one of those jobs to get ticked off early. A few tips:

- The rings you and your partner get don't need to match in colour, shape or style.

- Traditionally, your wedding ring goes under your engagement ring (closer to your heart), so be conscious of this when choosing a design.

- Your rings must be comfortable – remember, they're for a lifetime!

- Take your time searching for a jewellery designer who wants to understand the elements that are most important to you both.

The main point here is that your rings are going to be around forever. Take the time to get them right and look after them! Don't say I didn't warn you …

# GETTING STARTED

Now your engagement ring is clean, your goals are aligned and your budget is set. Here are the must-haves when planning your big day:

**Make a good spreadsheet.** You can opt to download a template or you can make it yourself, but whatever you do, you need to start it now. So many couples start with a planning journal, move onto a Word document, add some things into Pinterest and then get to a spreadsheet. Keep everything in one place!

**Create a wedding email address.** Keeping everything in one email is so much easier than hunting among your online shopping and spam emails for something the caterers said two years ago.

**Do your research.** Spend some time on social media, buy the wedding magazines, go to the wedding fayre. Use this time to figure out what you like and want. Make sure you have a good understanding of the day you want before booking big-ticket items like venues.

## Who's with you

Deciding who will be alongside you both when you get married is a huge consideration. Here are some questions you need to answer:

Who will be walking you down the aisle?

Who will be making speeches?

Who will be giving you the rings?

Are any children going to have roles?

Who will be in your bridal party?

My honest opinion is that you shouldn't lock in any of these decisions too early on. Make sure you are very clear about the type of wedding you're having before you commit to decisions about who will be involved. Doing a bridesmaid-proposal box looks cool on TikTok, but will you all still be friends in two years' time? 'Of course we will!' said all the brides who later had to cut bridesmaids from their wedding parties. My advice to you: don't ask them until you know your venue and budget at the very least.

# BRIDESMAIDS

What do they do? What can they pick? How do you manage them? Feel free to quote this part of the book to your bridal party – in fact, stick it into their bridesmaid-proposal boxes!

**Will you be a maid to the bride?**

**Will you help, support and guide the bride throughout her wedding planning and especially on the day?**

**Will you help as well as prop up the bar?**

OK, this doesn't quite have the same ring to it as 'Will you be my bridesmaid?', but make sure you're picking people who are actually going to be good at it.

## Good bridesmaid code of conduct

Thou shalt remember it's not about you. It's the bride's day and their time to be centre of attention. Champion the couple.

Thou shalt be a master of diplomacy. When mothers disagree with seating plans, it's your job to change the subject.

Thou shalt provide emotional support. Keep the bride calm, happy and excited. You are a shoulder to cry on and a hype girl all in one.

Thou shalt embrace the dress. It might not be what you would have picked, but it's not your wedding, so move on.

Thou shalt be active on messages. Engage in conversation, keep communication going and don't ghost on the hen-do chat.

Thou shalt dance like nobody is watching. Keep energy high on the wedding day: be fun, have fun and create fun.

## Who picks the bridesmaid dresses?

A general rule of thumb is that if you want to pick it, you pay for it. For example, if you want them to wear a certain colour or style, you're buying the dress. If you want their hair up/straight/curled, then you cover the costs – same with makeup. If budget allows, it's nice to cover all the above. Remember, it's an expensive time for bridesmaids too, with hen parties, travel to the wedding, accommodation, gifts and so on. Try not to add to the pressure with additional costs and fees.

**Top Tip:** Sell your bridesmaid dresses after the wedding!

As the bride, it's important to consider that this group are also still your friends, not just bridesmaids. You don't get the full attention for two years in the run-up to your big day. Take time out of wedding planning to check in on them too.

# GROOMSMEN

Well, this one may be a lot easier, but the same rules apply. Who is going to be helpful? Who does your partner want with them? Who will look good in a suit? The main question for the groomsmen is whether or not to buy the suit. Let's have a look at the pros and cons ...

## Pros

Uniformity: if you buy them, you get to pick them and they will all be matching

Suits can double up as wedding gifts

You can avoid any fashion mishaps with 'that' groomsman

## Cons

Weddings are expensive and buying suits for all can be costly

You can't dictate the exact suit they wear

You're not allowing the groomsmen a little room for individuality

Whether you have decided to buy suits, hire tuxes or let the groomsmen pick, it's necessary to have open and honest conversations right at the start. Ask your groomsmen for their thoughts ... Maybe even check their wardrobes!

My final point in this section is that while a father of the bride *typically* walks the bride down the aisle and does a speech, that doesn't mean he has to. Want your mum to walk you down? Want your dad to meet you halfway? Want your brother to do the speech? You can create roles for the people most important to you.

# THE DRESS

Hands up who is only worrying about the dress? Yep, been there. Firstly, let's start with the shape of dresses available to you, including silhouettes, necklines and waistlines.

**Now, it's time to go
dress shopping, so here are my
biggest tips for you:**

- Less is more. Don't take too many people. You'll want the opinions of your nearest and dearest, but more is definitely not merrier.

- Squat test. I know you want your ass to look good, but can you move? You need to be able to sit, dance and pee!

- Price tag. Ignore what Jessie J says, it absolutely is about the price tag. Be realistic with what you are comfortable spending and don't try on a dress that is thousands over budget.

- Open your mind. Try on all different styles of dress, not just the ones you think you'll like. You may surprise yourself.

- Book your venue before your dress! I'd argue the dress you pick for a church ceremony and grand castle in winter would be very different to a woodland blessing and tipi in summer.

# SILHOUETTES

| Mermaid | A-Line | Trumpet | Ball gown | Sheath |

# NECKLINES

| V-neck | Illusion | Halter | Scoop | Sweetheart | Off the shoulder |

# WAISTLINES

| Basque waist | Dropped waist | Empire | 'Natural' waist | Princess |

## Shopping list

When dress shopping, it's important to be prepared, so here's your pack list:

- Good underwear – shapewear, skin-toned and comfortable

- Heels – try to consider what heel height you'll be wearing and bring some with you

- Hair bands/clips – you may want to try out a few styles while picking your dress

- Strapless bra – be ready to test out different necklines

**Top Tip:** Do you want to change the vibe and have a bit more freedom to dance in the evening? Do you want to add a bit of sparkle? If this is something you want, then consider the budget and allow room for a second dress.

Finding and buying arguably the most important outfit you'll ever wear comes with a lot of pressure. Dress regret is a very real thing, so it's crucial to take your time to pick the right one. I suggest starting early to allow yourself enough time to browse without a deadline!

Most dresses require nine to twelve months to be made and shipped to your bridal store, so you will need to start shopping at least twelve months prior. If you leave it later than this, you may need to buy off the rack, which will give you less choice.

# GIFT IDEAS

Gifts aren't necessary, but if you are considering getting presents for your nearest and dearest then here are some of my favourite ideas ...

### Gifts for men (groom, fathers of the bride and groom, best man):

- Embroidered handkerchief
- Photo of you both
- Personalized washbag
- Alcohol – a personalized bottle of their favourite tipple
- A shared experience – for example, whisky tasting

### Gifts for women (bride, bridesmaids, mothers of the bride and groom)

- Locket with photos
- Jewellery – maybe with birthstones
- Photographs
- Candle
- A shared experience – for example, a spa day

However, the most important thing you can gift is a letter. Take some time to write down your thoughts and feelings for them to read the morning of the wedding.

# GETTING YOUR HEAD AROUND TIMINGS

Before you start planning in earnest, I have one major tip for you. I can almost guarantee that any less than enjoyable weddings you've been to would have suffered because of the timings. Did you have too long in the drinks reception and ran out of drinks? Was there a big lull after the wedding breakfast and you felt bored? Did it all finish way too early? The good thing about timings is that you can make these work for you!

Here's a super-quick guide to wedding day timings, but let's work our way through it. Before you contact a registrar or church and book a ceremony time, stop! You have got to know the timings you want before doing this. I have seen far too many couples book a 3 p.m. ceremony before working out that this means a 10 p.m. first dance! So even if it's a rough draft, plot your day.

**Ceremony**

Church + 1 hour
In ceremony + 30 minutes
Registrar + 30 minutes

**Confetti**

No confetti + none
In ceremony + none
Line + 15 minutes

**Travel**

No travel + none
Travel + **minutes

**Drinks reception**

Drinks + 1 hour
& Canapés + 1.5 hours
& Entertainment + 2 hours

**Guests to be seated**

Close by + 15 minutes
Interactive plan + 30 mins

**Speeches**

2 speeches + 20 minutes
3 speeches + 30 minutes
4 speeches + 45 minutes

**Wedding breakfast**

2 courses + 1.5 hours
3 courses + 2 hours
Always check with caterers

**Cocktail hour**

Band set-up + 1 hour/1.5 hours
Turnaround + 1 hour
No turnaround - 30 minutes

CHAPTER 2

# Elevate Your Day

Here's a whole load of
great ideas, tips and tricks
to get you started!

Let's get started on ways to really take the day from a wedding to *your* wedding. There is absolutely no point spending all this money on one day if it doesn't scream 'you'! Think about your personalities, your interests, your passions; how you met, what you've done, things you hate, things that would make your friends say, 'This is so them!' That is the biggest compliment you can have about your wedding. Be original, be different and be brave.

It would be near impossible for me to give personalized help in this book, so my job here is to get your ideas flowing. I can give you inspiration and examples, and the rest is over to you. If you're finding it hard to think of what you can do that's original, ask yourselves these questions:

How and where did you meet?

How do you spend your weekends?

Can you use music from the year you met?

Where did you get engaged?

What are your individual passions?

What do you do for work?

Where do you like to eat?

What do your friends think of first when they think of you?

If in doubt, ask your nearest and dearest – they may be able to give you ideas and spark memories that you just have to include. Here are some real wedding ideas that might inspire you:

- An older couple didn't want their guests to give money in a card but knew they would want to gift something. They asked guests to bring a record they thought the couple would enjoy!

- I personally met my now husband at TGI Fridays. We had a celebrant ceremony on our wedding day, so on the legal wedding day we had our wedding breakfast at that very same restaurant – classy, I know.

- One bride who had unfortunately lost her mother before her wedding had a message from her late mum embroidered into the veil.

- A football-mad bride and groom created a logo that incorporated both their teams and the day had little sprinklings of football throughout.

- A groom proposed to his partner by having a personalized menu made at their favourite restaurant, with the words 'Will you marry me?' on the back. These personalized menus will be a big feature on their wedding tables.

# WEDDING STATIONERY

Personalized stationery is the easiest way to add personality and fun to your wedding day. Here is a list of all the stationery you could need:

- Reserved signs
- Welcome sign
- 'Unplugged ceremony' sign
- Order of the day
- Table plan
- Name cards
- Table names/numbers
- Menus
- Newspapers
- Strut cards (little stand-up signs) for things like signature cocktails or a prop shop
- Table talkers (little trifold stand-up cards) for things such as bar menus or table games
- Vow books
- Reading cards
- Backing cards for speeches

You can add quotes, pictures, sayings, themes, characters –
anything at all! Think 'Nana's favourite lemon drizzle cake' or
'Monty's Mojitos'. Stationery is also a very easy one to DIY.
Whether you design it and have it printed or make it yourself at
home, it's a good cost saver!

**Top Tip:** Use the same font across all stationery to make your
wedding look more luxurious – match it to your invitations and
you're basically a graphic designer!

## Whose name goes first?

Ensure that you use the same name order throughout the wedding.
Are you Brian & Georgie or Georgie & Brian? Decide which and
stick to it on your invites, stationery and logo, so they all tie in.

## To apostrophe or not to apostrophe?

If you're having a neon sign or any sign that says something along
the lines of 'The Mitchells', you never have an apostrophe.

If your surname ends with an s, x, z, ch or sh, you add 'es' – for
example, 'The Davises'. If your surname ends with anything else, you
just add an s – for example, 'The Smiths'.

Unfortunately, some surnames don't look pretty with the 'es', so you
may have to opt for 'Mr & Mrs Davies' instead!

# FORGOTTEN ITEMS

Here's my list of things couples always forget to check or arrange:

- Pens for the guestbook
- Highchairs
- Bins
- Decor that can be dotted around to help tie everything together
- Boxes to take decor away in afterwards
- A box for cards
- Cake platters
- Cake knife

# JARGON BUSTER

- **MoH** – maid of honour

- **FoB** – father of the bride

- **MoB** – mother of the bride

- **FoG** – father of the groom

- **MoG** – mother of the groom

- **BM** – best man

- **Drinks reception** – after the ceremony, before the meal

- **Wedding breakfast** – the main sit-down meal

- **Turnaround** – the time when a space is changed from the ceremony/day to party/night

- **Corkage** – a charge for providing your own drinks at a wedding

- **Civil ceremony** – a legal ceremony (registrars)

- **Celebrant** – a person who marries you (not legal in England, Wales or Ireland)

- **Favours** – a small gift on each person's place setting

- **Charger plates** – decorative plates, similar to placemats (not for food)

- **Flat lay** – an image taken from above of accessories (such as perfume, invitation, rings)

- **Buttonhole** – a small flower put on a suit jacket

- **Corsage** – a women's flower, usually worn on the wrist, jacket or bag

- **Bustle** – a way to shorten your train, usually by buttoning it up

- **Sweetheart table** – a top table just for two

- **Master of ceremonies (MC)** – the person who makes your announcements throughout the day

CHAPTER 3

# The Ceremony

# I do ... want to know more about the ceremony!

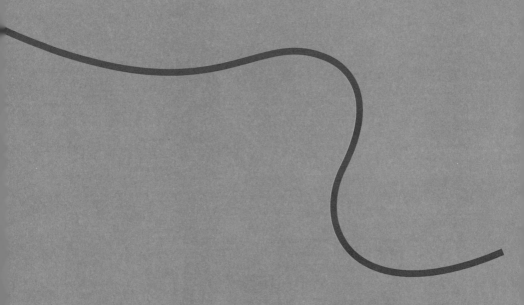

So here it is, the ceremony. The moment that makes this party a wedding. Your ceremony is the first impression guests will have, so make sure you take some time to think about how you want it to look and feel. Do you want it to be a celebration of your love so far? Do you want it to be funny, romantic, classy? Talk together to understand what you want from this time and prioritize making this bit all about you two.

Ceremonies can look different, and you absolutely have some scope to make it personal, even if you opt for a legal ceremony. Let me talk you through the steps for the most 'typical' ceremony, so you can understand the standard format.

1. The groom is stood at the front of the ceremony with the best man/groomsmen.

2. The registrar introduces themselves (there are actually two: one to conduct the ceremony and one to sign the documents), asks guests to refrain from using phones and explains they are here to legally marry the couple.

3. The registrars are given the thumbs up and then ask guests to be upstanding.

4. The music starts and the bridal party makes its entrance.

5. The bride enters with the FoB.

6. Guests are asked to be seated (the FoB and BM remain standing).

7. The registrar makes a statement and asks who gives this woman away – the FoB will then be seated along with the BM.

8. The registrar reads out a legal statement about marriage.

9. A guest does a reading.

10. Legal declarations are made, with the couple asked to repeat the phrases.

11. A guest does a reading.

12. The wedding vows and promises are made.

13. Rings are exchanged.

14. The kiss is announced.

15. The register is signed (while the couple are seated) with witnesses.

16. The couple stand back at the front and the second registrar comes forward to give the certificate of marriage.

17. The registrar gives their congratulations and announces the couple as married.

18. Exit.

This is a very broad and stereotypical example of the most common type of ceremony. However, when you're planning your day, keep in mind that every location, registrar and wedding is different. For legal weddings, you will be given choices about what to say in the ceremony – the famous example being whether you want to say, 'I obey you.' I absolutely didn't want to agree to that!

**Top Tip:** At a legal ceremony, you will sit and sign the register after you've been announced as married and have shared your first kiss – so don't start leaving until that's done.

- Change who you walk down the aisle with – for example, do you want to meet your partner outside and walk in together?

- Don't want any readings? Cut them out.

- Want your guests to take photos in the ceremony? Let them.

- Want to sing a song midway through? Check if the registrars are game.

# CELEBRANT VERSUS LEGAL WEDDING

First things first, what's the difference? Ceremonies have different rules depending on the country you are marrying in. Remember that episode of *Friends* where Joey gets ordained so he can marry Monica and Chandler? That will pass in the US but not in England, I'm afraid. In England, the only people who can marry you outside of a church are registrars.

With a legal wedding, you don't get to pick the person who will conduct the ceremony and you don't get a huge amount of choice in what is said. However, it is all signed, sealed and delivered right there. These are the most common ceremonies in England and the usual route that couples go down.

If you are looking for a more personal approach, you can choose to have a friend, family member or a celebrant marry you, but you'll need to do the legal part another time. The positives are that you get to pick the person conducting your wedding, you dictate the script and make your own rules, and it can be exactly how you picture it to be.

You can decide to make the legal part of your wedding as big or as small as you wish. Some couples choose to just go and sign the documents with their witnesses, while others want a little bit more. For example, you may choose to have a legal ceremony with a select group of friends and family, followed by a party at the pub, or you could go back to the place you met your partner for photographs and champagne. This is your chance to have an extra wedding day, totally different from your 'proper' wedding day – because if you're already planning one wedding, you might as well do two. Alternatively, you can opt to just sign the paperwork – in this case, think of it like registering a birth: the birthday is the event you remember, while the paperwork is a formality.

**Top Tip:** If you have a registrar in England or an officiant in America, you will both need to be interviewed before the ceremony. Person one (usually the groom) will be interviewed around thirty minutes before the ceremony and person two (usually the bride) will be interviewed fifteen minutes before and then go straight down the aisle.

# CEREMONY SEATING PLAN

I know being asked to create a seating plan for the ceremony may make you want to close this book, but hear me out. It's not for all the guests, just a few. Having reserved signs in your ceremony is non-negotiable and let me tell you why ... I'll set the scene: it's a gorgeous ceremony, your guests are all waiting, the music starts, tears begin to flow and your bridesmaids make their way down the aisle. They get to the front and find there are no seats for them; they look confused, then walk back up the aisle, squeeze past Uncle Dave and take some random empty seats. *No, thank you!*

Reserved signs are crucial for anyone who will be walking down the aisle. They ensure there will be seats available for them at the front so you can avoid that awkward backward shuffle. So, at the bare minimum you'll need reserved seats for the bridesmaids, the father of the bride (or whoever is walking you down the aisle), flower girls, page boys ... You get the gist.

I would also recommend having seats reserved for super-close family. This helps your mother-in-law feel special, and we want to keep her happy. It's also a good idea to have seats for anyone who is doing a reading or is a witness – preferably on the aisle so they can get up easier.

My final tip on reserved signs is to write people's names on them. I have seen too many weddings where they just say 'Reserved', so everyone avoids them and there ends up being two rows of empty seats at the front. If your nan is like my nan, she won't want to make a fuss and will assume she's at the back. Or worse, your great auntie will assume she is special enough for a reserved sign and will sit herself front and centre! Below I have popped an example for reserved seating. Yours may look nothing like this, and that's OK – mine didn't either. It's just food for thought.

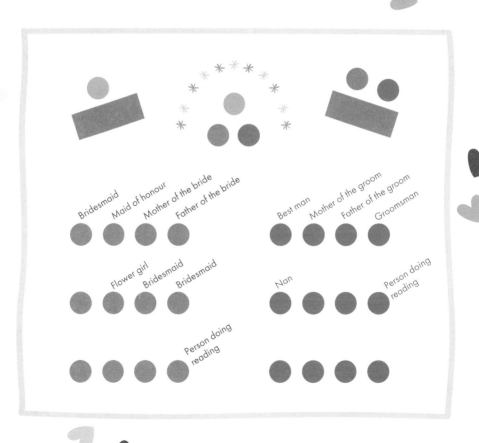

# LAYOUT

If you are having a legal ceremony, you will have two registrars. One will sit during the ceremony to write the legal parts (table on the left) and one will stand and conduct the ceremony.

After you have said your vows and exchanged rings you will sit to sign the wedding certificate (table on the right). You may want to keep this in mind when thinking about the space and furniture needed for a ceremony. If you are having a celebrant ceremony, you can decide to do a symbolic signing and have the same set-up.

You will also need to work out how many chairs you'd like in each row and keep this in mind for your seating plan.

## Spice up your ceremony

There are lots of options for ceremony layouts if you're looking for something a little different. I've done weddings with curved layouts, or circular with the couple marrying in the middle – or there's the more recent trend of runway aisles.

It's very rare these days for guests to be asked to pick whose side to sit on. It certainly used to be common to have the bride's family on the left side and the groom's on the right. However, more and more couples are choosing layouts that mean their families can see their faces, or are swapping the families' sides.

If you picture yourselves facing each other to say your vows, do you want your family behind your partner, so they can see you, or do you want to keep it traditional? Alternatively – and here's another opportunity for me to talk about my own wedding – we asked our celebrant to conduct some of the ceremony from the middle of the aisle so we were facing our guests and everyone could see us.

# THE THREE S's
# FOR GROOMSMEN

**Say hello.** This is an obvious one but it's easy to forget. Make sure your groom and groomsmen greet guests. Have someone standing at the first point of entrance ready to direct guests to the ceremony space. The groom should be in the ceremony room saying hello when people arrive there.

**Saved seats.** You should already have some reserved signs down, but make sure the groomsmen know about them and who will be sitting where. That way, they can help seat guests as they enter and ensure the important people get their seats.

**Scooch over.** Empty aisle seats will make the ceremony room look empty in photographs, so get your groomsmen to ensure people scooch over and fill them.

# UNPLUGGED CEREMONIES

An unplugged ceremony basically means no electronics, aka no pictures. I'm going to pull the professional card here and say that I highly recommend you have an unplugged ceremony, and my reasons are threefold:

1.  The last thing you or your photographer want is Uncle Dave getting his iPad in the way of the proper photographs (the ones you've paid for).
2.  You want to be able to see your guests' faces in the pictures, without them hidden behind a phone.
3.  It's nice to keep this part of the day just for you and your guests: let everyone be truly present.

If you do want guests to stay off their phones, I would ask whoever is conducting your ceremony to tell them so before it starts. Alternatively, you can have a friendly welcome sign that lets them know.

A nice touch is having your celebrant (or groomsmen) tell guests to send you guys a photo and a good-luck message before the ceremony begins. This helps with people's desperation to take photos and is a win-win because you get to read all the lovely messages the next day!

# WALKING DOWN THE AISLE: WHO, WHAT, WHEN ...

Now this is a super-personal choice and there's not a huge amount of advice I can give you about who to pick, but what *normally* happens is ...

Your flower girls and page boys will walk down first (a reserved sign for their parents is a good idea so they can be sitting near the front somewhere).

Next up are bridesmaids. Depending on how many you want and how long the entrance will be, you can have them walk down together in pairs, or one at a time. Some people go down the more American route and have bridesmaids and groomsmen walk in together.

Last but by no means least, you will walk down the aisle with whoever you decide. Let's assume for the sake of this section it's your dad. You will want your dad to be on your left because your groom will be on the right of you when you get to the front – an easy way to remember this is: **'Left Dad behind, marrying Mr Right.'**

When it's your turn to walk, pause just at the start of the aisle. Enjoy that moment, take it all in, take a big breath and then go – *slowly*. I would recommend a good five-second stop here. This is also a great point for your partner to turn around and see you in all your glory!

# MUSIC

If you are like me, the music will be the bit that sets the tears off. It's important to get this bit right, so here's what you need to know about ceremony music. If budget allows, live music hits hard – string quartets, piano, violins ... anything would be amazing. If your budget doesn't allow, then don't worry; just make sure the venue has a good sound system and that you've nailed your playlists. You're going to need four playlists for the ceremony:

**Pre-ceremony.** This is a group of songs for when guests are arriving. Think acoustic covers, soft romantic vibes or something that's a bit of you! I would recommend an hour's worth of music here to be safe.

**Walking down the aisle.** This is the hardest music choice you will ever make. Some people know what they'll use the minute they get engaged, but for others it's not so obvious. My advice would be that if telling people what it is doesn't make you ridiculously excited, then it's not the one.

I walked down the aisle to the *Friends* theme tune – an acoustic version, of course. My husband and I have watched the TV show throughout our relationship and often go to sleep with it playing in the background, so it felt very us.

People usually need just one song for this bit – but some decide to have their bridal party walk down to one song and themselves to another, so that's certainly an option. I would consider how long the

aisle is, how many people you have walking down the aisle and how long the song or songs last.

**Signing the register.** If you are having a legal ceremony (or doing a symbolic signing), you'll need some music to play during this part. Usually, you'll need two songs, but I always recommend putting one more in, just in case. Again, this is a little opportunity to put a bit of personality into your day, so pick music that means something to you both. One wedding had their string quartet play the *Match of the Day* theme tune as a little nod to the football-loving groom.

**Exiting.** You'll need a song for your walk back out together, so make it good. You should try to choose something a bit more uplifting, and you'll want it loud – hopefully everyone will be clapping and whooping, so high energy is good.

**Top Tip:** If someone is playing your ceremony music from a playlist, you'll want to avoid it stopping abruptly when you arrive at the top of the aisle – so ask them to 'slow fade' when you get there.

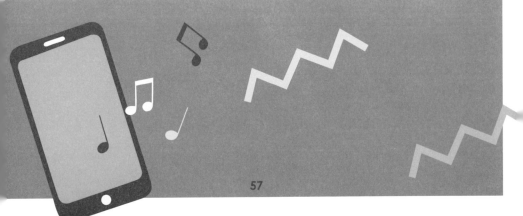

# DECOR

It's important to get this right and find the balance. The ceremony lasts only thirty minutes, but it is the first impression of the day and where a good chunk of your photos will be taken. I suggest you go for a focal point in the ceremony, whether that's a broken arch, floral display, candles or a feature frame – it's good to have something that draws the eye and will frame your photographs.

You can then look at adding some decor down the aisle, so petals are good, pew ends and candles (but please do consider how wide the aisle is and how likely your dress is to set on fire! If you're worried, go LEDs).

**Top Tip:** Make sure you reuse your decor! If anything can be moved from the ceremony room to somewhere else, then do it. Or if your ceremony room is being turned around to the wedding breakfast room, then even easier. I have worked with many couples who have used their table centrepieces in the ceremony room – things like bud vases or lanterns. Your florist or coordinator will help with this.

## Signage

Signage can be ordered through a stationery company, or you can design items yourselves and get them professionally printed. I always think a welcome sign gives guests a good first impression, acts as a nice photo backdrop and lets everyone know they are in the right place. It can then be moved to another area of the venue for use all day. For this section of the day, you could also consider:

- Reserved signs – essential for your wedding ceremony.

- Unplugged-ceremony sign – this makes it clear if you don't quite trust your guests to get the memo.

- Order-of-the-day sign – so people know what's happening when.

If you're a Type-A bride known for your lists and plans, you can have great fun displaying your order of the day. Think about how you can get creative and let your personality shine through.

**2 p.m.** Get married

**4 p.m.** Speeches

**4.30 p.m.** Wedding breakfast

**7 p.m.** First dance

**9 p.m.** More food!

**2 a.m.** It's time for bed

**Top Tip:** Have your card box somewhere in your ceremony or entrance room – nobody wants to be holding on to a card all through the ceremony.

# READINGS

Unless you really want a quick ceremony, I'd highly recommend having readings. Picking the perfect one can be difficult, but here is another opportunity to showcase a little personality – and lucky for you, I have some tips!

- This is a nice job to make someone feel involved in the day – so think about who might enjoy it.

- Be original! Do not just google 'readings for weddings'; this is boring, and nobody wants a boring ceremony. Find things that aren't readings – look for quotes from films, poems, song lyrics, TV wedding readings ... anything but 'Love is patient'!

- Make it personal. Write your own reading, get someone to write a poem about you, use marriage advice from family members. Find something that strikes a chord.

I had four readings – two at the legal one and two at the wedding:

- A quote from Lucas Scott in *One Tree Hill*

- A poem of one-liners from *Friends*

- A personal poem that our celebrant wrote and our daughter read

- Jordan Peterson's quote about margaritas on a beach

Every one of them means something to us, individually or as a couple. Do not stop looking for a reading until you've found something that feels 100 per cent right.

# CHILDREN

Let me just say (in case my daughter ever reads this book in the future) that I love children; they are wonderful and add a spark to weddings ... However, kids talking, crying or moaning in a ceremony is not a vibe! Too many times I have seen children get bored, fidgety, start chatting and asking questions and then their parents were unable to concentrate, the couple couldn't hear, the person conducting the ceremony needed to speak louder and it was just awkward.

So please do not feel bad for suggesting to parents beforehand that if their children are fussy, they can please feel free to take them out of the room. We had little order-of-service newspapers and I included a note that said:

# Requests from the bride & groom:

'Hey kiddos, can you hear the bells?
Time to quiet those noisy yells.
Zip your lips and take a seat,
Or we'll hide all the
wedding treats!'

I have also seen weddings where children were looked after in
a different room so the parents could be fully present.

# THE BEST-MAN NUDGE

Have you discussed when you want your partner to turn to look at you during the ceremony? The best moment for you to be seen in all your glory is at the start of the aisle, when you have paused before starting your walk. However, when you're a little closer might be easier for more nervous grooms. Either way, the best man should be ready to give them a little nudge at the right moment, so they know to turn. It's one of the best parts of the whole day!

# RINGS

It's good to practise how to put on your wedding rings. Typically, your best man will present you with the rings and you will take each other's. Hold the ring midway down the fourth finger on the left hand and repeat the promises – then slide the ring on. Hold the ring with one hand and their palm with your other – this looks best for photos.

# FINISHING TOUCHES

Just a few things to think about adding to your ceremony:

- Ring box – this will be in photos so is worth the £10.

- Tissues – you can get lovely personalized ones for the chairs.

- Orders of service – you'll want these for your church ceremony but could still include them at other venues.

- Reading and vow books – you won't want people reading from screwed-up bits of paper or, even worse, phones! (I recommend making covers for them so they look good in the photographs. I printed mine at home and added some ribbon: bargain!)

Three ways to include people in your wedding ... without making them bridesmaids!

1. Have them do a reading during your ceremony – this is a lovely job for the more confident guest you want to include.

2. Ask them to be your witness. Even for a celebrant ceremony, you can have a certificate and ask them to sign it.

3. Ask them to be your 'something blue'. This is a really lovely way to make people feel special! Buy them a blue dress or blue jewellery and write them a nice letter about how much you love them and need them to be there on your big day.

## Don't forget to SMILE …

**S**eats. Ask your groomsmen to make sure guests don't avoid the aisle seats. The natural reaction is for guests to move up to make space, but you don't want to look like you've got no friends.

**M**iddle. Please, just for me, make sure you are both in the centre of the aisle. You'll be so sad when you see photos and you're off to the left.

**I**'m looking. See best-man's nudge – decide together at what point you want your partner to look at you walking down the aisle. Is it when you're right at the start, or when you're close together?

**L**ong kiss. Kiss long enough for your photographer to get the shot, but not too long that your nan has to look away.

**E**xit big. Enjoy walking back out together as a newly married couple! Stop in the middle for a kiss, high-five people, throw your bouquet in the air – just celebrate!

# Georgie's Timing Tips

Picking your ceremony time can be difficult and is something couples often do straight after their venue visit. Make sure you know your whole day's plans before booking a 12 p.m. ceremony! Equally, don't waste the day by saying 3 p.m.

For ceremony durations, the general rule of thumb is:

## Church ceremonies
Usually one hour (unless you opt for Nuptial Mass, which is one and a half hours). I recommend speaking to your vicar or priest to gauge accurate timings based on how many hymns and readings you'll be having.

## Registrar ceremonies
Thirty minutes is usually allocated, but these can be as short as twenty minutes when there are no readings and you opt for a quick ceremony.

## Celebrant ceremonies
These are harder to guess, but the majority are also around thirty minutes. I opted to have an additional ring exchange, two readings and vows with my daughter ('cause I'm extra), so it was more like forty-five minutes. Again, I'd recommend speaking to your celebrant to get a better idea.

Here are the two most popular timings for weddings in the UK (church versus venue):

## VENUE

**2 p.m.** ceremony

**2.30 p.m.** confetti and photos

**2.45 p.m.** drinks reception, canapés, photos, music

**4.15 p.m.** guests to be seated

**4.30 p.m.** speeches (x three)

**5 p.m.** wedding breakfast (three-course meal)

**7 p.m.** cake cutting, guests to move out, turnaround

**7 p.m.** cocktail hour

**7.30 p.m.** evening guests arrive

**8 p.m.** first dance

**10 p.m.** evening food

**12 p.m.** guests to depart

## CHURCH

**1 p.m.** ceremony

**2 p.m.** confetti and photos

**2.15 p.m.** guests depart

**2.45 p.m.** guests arrive, drinks reception, canapés, photos, music

**4.15 p.m.** guests to be seated

**4.30 p.m.** speeches (x three)

**5 p.m.** wedding breakfast (three-course meal)

**7 p.m.** cake cutting, guests to move out, turnaround

**7 p.m.** cocktail hour

**7.30 p.m.** evening guests arrive

**8 p.m.** first dance

**10 p.m.** evening food

**12 p.m.** guests to depart

If you want to have an earlier or later ceremony time, you will just need to consider the timings that follow. Maybe you're having more speeches? Maybe you want a shorter drinks reception? Maybe you need to finish at the venue earlier? Well, before you get excited and book that 12 p.m. ceremony, remember that if you're getting ready somewhere fifteen minutes away and have five bridesmaids, you may well be looking at a 5 a.m. start time. The most important factors to consider are:

- You need to be ready one hour before your ceremony (to allow for first looks, photos and buffer time)

- Hair and makeup usually take one hour per person, per supplier (one hour for hair, one hour for makeup)

- Do you need to travel to the ceremony? (If so, how long will it take?)

- Are you having a legal ceremony and therefore need an interview with the registrar? (If so, allow fifteen minutes before your ceremony.)

**Top Tip:** Some hair and makeup artists offer to bring additional suppliers with them. This allows you to have more bridal-party members done in a shorter amount of time.

## Travel

Are you getting married at a different location to the reception venue? Then don't forget the travel time. Church weddings, registry offices or ceremony venues may all require transport or travel time in between, and again be realistic.

**Top Tip:** If guests are getting on a bus, make sure you have a bridesmaid or groomsman in charge of telling guests where to go and supporting them. Some weddings even have a tick list to ensure everyone is there.

Make sure you allow time for guests to make their way to the bus/their cars and drive to the venue and park. For example, if the church is ten minutes from the venue, allow a more realistic fifteen minutes. I recommend telling your venue/caterer/bar the earliest time guests will arrive, to ensure they are ready for you.

# CONFETTI

You have two options if you want confetti – you can set up a confetti line after the ceremony, or you can get guests to throw it as you walk back down the aisle. Here are my thoughts on both options ...

## Confetti line

This is my personal favourite and is for the couples who really want that full confetti moment. The plan is this: you will be announced and enjoy walking back down the aisle hand in hand and head off to an area away from the guests – this will stop everyone coming over to congratulate you and therefore taking up thirty minutes of your drinks reception!

In the meantime, your coordinator, venue manager or bridesmaids will encourage guests to make two lines. Your venue will usually have a place they recommend for this, or you can decide where looks good – either side of a path, the entrance to the venue or near the ceremony work well. You can then both walk together down the middle and thoroughly enjoy that moment – the longer the line the better! Then you can head off to grab a drink and guests will follow.

## Aisle confetti

If you're looking for less fuss and an easier exit, this is a good option for you; likewise, this is good if your ceremony space is the perfect photo backdrop. The downside is that only the guests on the aisle seats will be able to throw your confetti.

I recommend having confetti in bags that you pop on chairs before the ceremony and tell your celebrant or registrar when you want guests to throw it. When you reach the end of the aisle, you can head straight off to start the reception drinks.

Given the unpredictability of weather, I suggest having a few alternative plans in place:

- **Plan A** – outside, after the ceremony.

- **Plan B** – find another point later in the day (for example, before being called into dinner) to go back outside.

- **Plan C** – if it's going to rain all day, go for aisle confetti or a smaller confetti throw with your bridal party, featuring umbrellas, or even during your first dance.

# TIPS FOR CONFETTI

## Don't forget NESW (north, east, south, west) ...

**N**o nasty faces! When guests are throwing confetti at you, your natural reaction will likely be to scrunch your eyes closed, pull faces and cover your mouth – but don't! Nice, natural faces please.

**E**yes up! Try not to look at the floor the whole time – keep your head high and look forward, at guests and at your partner.

**S**top for kisses! Do this at the start, halfway through and at the end of the confetti line. Kisses look great in photos and stopping for them allows your photographer to capture them.

**W**alk slowly! Again, this gives your content team time to capture the moments (remember, they are walking backwards) as well as allowing your guests to actually throw the confetti. Enjoy the walk.

## Traditional confetti types

- Paper confetti is perfect for 'that' confetti shot. It falls slowly, is cost-effective and comes in a variety of colour combinations.

- Petals are more eco-friendly, smell gorgeous and give that spring country-garden wedding feel.

- Foil confetti is quite hard to come by as it's typically not biodegradable. I'd save this for the dancefloor.

## Bags or baskets?

Bags (on seats) work well if you're having confetti as you walk back down the aisle. If you're aiming to have the confetti line, I recommend just popping it all into a basket so it's easier for guests to grab (and saves you the time and cost of bags!). You can never have too much confetti!

**Top Tip:** If you're looking to have a whole-group photo, do it straight after confetti while you have everyone's attention.

## Confetti timing

If you decide to have confetti during the ceremony, you won't need any additional time. For the traditional confetti line, it will probably take about ten to fifteen minutes to get everyone ready and do your walk, so it's good to ensure you allow time for this.

# CHAPTER 4

# The Drinks Reception

# How to start your
# wedding right ...

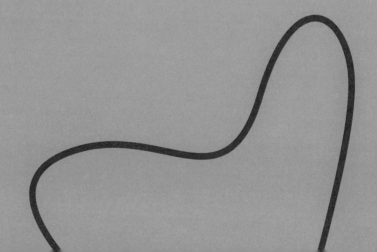

At this point in the day, your guests will expect to be handed a free drink or two. Most drinks packages will offer something along the lines of prosecco and beer, but in my opinion it's good to spice it up a little. Here's another first impression that your guests will absolutely remember from the day.

# DRINKS

Personality is key, so think about the drinks you like. Can you serve them in a fun way? Can you add cute signs? Can you use local drinks? Here are some of my favourite ways to keep it cool ...

## Signature cocktails

You can start to personalize your wedding straight away with signature cocktails, also known as 'his and hers cocktails'. A few of my favourites are:

Pornstar martini      Long Island iced tea

Dark and stormy      Rum punch

Espresso martini      Sex on the beach

Whisky sour      Mai tai

I recommend adding a nice little sign telling guests what the options are. Something along the lines of 'His Favourite' and 'Her Favourite'.

You might also want to have a Pimp Your Prosecco station, which lets guests spice up their drinks with ingredients such as orange juice, candyfloss, strawberries and cordial. You'll need tongs, jars, drink stirrers and napkins ... and it's a great opportunity for another sign.

## Beers

Stereotypically speaking, guys like beers. So, setting up a bathtub or buckets full of beer always goes down well.

**Top Tip:** Tie a bottle opener to the tub with string so it won't go wandering.

## Soft drinks

Don't forget about your non-drinking guests. Elderflower is a great option and still looks nice, but it's also worth thinking about the adults who may want alcohol-free beer or no-secco.

I recommend having a hydration station for water, too, which should be available all day long – especially in summer! There is nothing worse than having to queue at the bar just to grab a water. Set out a few simple Kilner-type jars with water and add a few slices of lemon/cucumber/mint sprigs to make it classy.

## Drink accessories

These might not yet be on your radar, but I'm about to put them there.

**Drinks toppers.** These are little paper discs that sit on top of cocktails, usually with a personalized logo, image, date or message (such as 'Sip, sip, hooray').

**Drink charms.** These are usually little plastic or metal charms – often initials – that sit on the edge of your glasses and look gorgeous.

**Personalized coasters.** Like the drinks toppers, you can put any message on these for a nice touch.

**Don't touch my drink.** These are like coasters but used by guests to show the venue that they don't want their drink to be cleared up. They can say something along the lines of 'Please don't take my drink – I'm lighting up the dancefloor.'

## Drinks station

This is another part of the planning that often gets overlooked. How are you serving these drinks? I recommend starting by speaking to your venue/caterer/bar – whoever is in charge of serving drinks – and see what they usually do. If it's boring, feel free to add to it. For example:

- Make a little effort with the table. Add jars with fruit, a little bud vase of flowers, signage – anything that takes it from boring to glorious.

- Scrap the table altogether. Go for something a little different like a ladder, drinks cart, canoe – you name it, it can work!

- Opt for tray service. If you're going for a more luxurious feel, having drinks served might be more on-brand.

## Quantities

If you're trying to work out how much booze is the right amount, I'm here to help ...

- On average (and again, this is just an idea of what's typical), guys will drink around three bottled beers per hour. Women will drink roughly one and a half glasses of prosecco per hour.

- A two-hour drinks reception with one hundred guests (fifty men and fifty women) = 300 beers and 150 glasses (twenty-five bottles) of prosecco.

- Cocktails are like prosecco, with guests drinking between one and a half to two per hour.

If you have the choice to have the bar available during this time, I'd say do it. Then guests who don't like the available options, have drunk their allocation or just want some variety can buy their own.

# CANAPÉS

Canapés are arguably the best part of a wedding! They are usually served throughout the drinks reception, starting around fifteen minutes after drinks have been served. They are often handed out on boards by the catering staff.

If you've had a ceremony any time between 11 a.m. and 3 p.m., then your guests are going to be hungry. You will be able to enjoy your drinks reception much more if you know your guests are being fed, watered and entertained. At a minimum you need to give your guests at least four canapés per person, but honestly the more the merrier. If canapés aren't your jam, here are a few alternative ideas:

- Scrap the canapés and set out a graze station. Guests can help themselves throughout the drinks reception – think breads, olives, meats, cheeses and dips. Set out little plates or bowls for self-service, add some decor and, of course, a sign – I had little food pots on our graze table that said, 'I'm only here for the food.'

- Fun food options such as a crisp wall, a doughnut wall or a popcorn bar.

- Cocktails and wedding cake! Handing out your wedding cake also ensures it gets eaten.

- Entertaining food options like an ice-cream cart, an oyster shucker or a coffee and doughnut van.

Don't forget to cater for dietary requirements! I would suggest having some meat, vegetarian, fish, hot and cold options. And finally, if your budget doesn't allow for both, I would recommend scrapping the starters to have canapés instead! In my opinion, they are appreciated more, fill the gap, act as a form of entertainment and keep guests full while you're having photos.

# MAKE IT PERSONAL

There are lots of opportunities to make your wedding fun, interesting and memorable without changing the flow of the day ...

- **Rename your drinks!** If you're opting to have cocktails, you can personalize their names. Marry Me Mimosas? What about a Georgie's Gimlet or a Bride's Bay Breeze?

- **Met in a nightclub?** What was the drink of choice that night? Can the test-tube shots make a comeback?

- **Engaged in Paris?** Where's the macarons at? Are there any French-themed canapés?

- **Film buff?** Set up a popcorn bar for guests to help themselves to. Add jars with different flavours, popcorn boxes, scoops, toppings – this will keep everyone entertained and happy.

# ENTERTAINMENT

We've lined their stomachs, the drinks are flowing … You'd think they'd be happy with this, but no – they'll want more.

Entertainment is a great way to set the tone for your wedding day. Is it a festival wedding? Going for a formal affair? Want it to feel like the party has started straight away? This is what entertainment can do. There are literally hundreds of options for this, so let's talk through the most popular …

## Music

Live music will always be a big hit and sets the tone for a gorgeous reception. It is also a great way to add some personality into your day. Some ideas to think about:

- Are you huge fan of classical music? Book a string quartet.

- Met at a gig? Play that music.

- Born in the Caribbean? Have steel drums.

- Started dating in 2012? Play music from that era.

- Taylor Swift lover? Get a tribute act.

String quartet, saxophonist, singer, acoustic guitar, cello, piano, violin, roaming band – they all work perfectly. It's also worth thinking about who was there for the ceremony, because very often the same musician can play during the drinks reception too.

If budget doesn't allow for live music, you will still need to have music playing. Pick a playlist that is sentimental to you both or fits the vibe – background music is essential. This also means you'll need to make sure you have speakers, a phone to play the music from and someone in charge of hitting play (this is usually the venue).

## Garden games

These are a big yes from me – an easy, cost-effective addition to the day where guests can choose to play if they like or opt out if it's not their thing; it's not mandatory.

## Live illustrations

Have an artist come and do drawings of guests, caricatures or little snippets of the day. These can act as lovely keepsakes for you or favours for your guests.

## Magic

Now, magic is different these days, so stop picturing a bunny being pulled from a hat. Think more close-up card tricks, mind games and illusions – definitely a crowd pleaser.

## Animals

Believe it or not, this is quite a popular choice. I've seen, in the space of one year, a petting zoo, an alpaca bride and groom, a horse and carriage and dog chaperones.

## Mini-golf

A miniature crazy-golf course set with themed holes, score cards and a leader board can be lots of fun.

## Football goal

Before you veto it, the ones I've seen have been great fun. You'd be surprised how much entertainment a ball and goal can give a group of guys.

## Organized games

Looking for a free option? A game of rounders, a rugby throw-around and sports-day themed races are all things that I've personally seen work really well.

I have said it before, and I'll say it again: entertainment provides another great opportunity to personalize your day. It's these choices that take your wedding from just anybody's day to yours.

Arguably entertainment is not essential and I do recommend allocating your budget to other things first, but it's definitely good to have some if you can. Keeping your guests entertained while you are greeting guests and having photos taken means you can enjoy yourself knowing they are well looked after.

**Top Tip:** Do you have a Plan A and Plan B for your drinks reception? Fingers crossed it's a beautiful day, but weather is unpredictable so you should ensure you have multiple options. When you look at potential venues, you need to consider their inside spaces as well as the grounds. Find out what spaces you would use if the ceremony room were being turned around and the weather was bad. It's also worth considering whether any decor or seating would be required in that space.

# PHOTOS

THIS IS THE LEAST EXCITING PART OF THE DAY. I don't mean to shout, but I cannot stress this enough – this bit sucks.

## Whole-group photograph

First things first. Let me give you the pros and cons for this:

### Pros

A whole-group photo is a way to guarantee you get a photo of every single guest at your wedding

Having everyone there makes it easy to then gather the people you need and move into the smaller group photos

It allows time for the drinks to be ready for service or the ceremony room to be cleared

### Cons

You can't really see every guest properly

It's a bitch of a photo to get – nobody listens

It delays the start of your drinks reception

If you're undecided, I'd say if you have fewer than sixty guests then go for it; if you have more than 120 then absolutely don't. For anything in between, it's up to you!

## Group photos

These are the photos you ask your photographer for, which include groups of family or friends, often taken during the drinks reception. As the couple, you will want to stay in one place and let guests join you then leave when their photos have been done.

Here's what you need to remember for your shot list:

**Write names, not relationship (Katrina, not Mum)**

**Make a note of how many people should be in the photo (x9)**

**It takes about five minutes per group, so pick wisely (max 8–10)**

**As the couple, you don't move!**

Remember, your photographer won't know who guests are, so the more support you can give them the quicker it will be. It's also important to make sure they and your other suppliers are aware of any family politics. I've seen many weddings where sworn enemies

Mum and Dad are put together but haven't seen each other in ten years (I've been guilty of this mistake myself)! To avoid any awkward moments, let us know in advance.

**Top Tip:** Ahead of the day, pick a person each who knows your side of the family and give them a printed list of who will be in each group picture, so they can tick it off and support your photographer.

I personally recommend getting the group photos done asap, but some suppliers will disagree – so take their lead or have this discussion. I think it's good to get them done straight after confetti, so guests don't wander off too far. However, if you feel you might need a drink and a minute to say hi, then opt to delay them slightly.

My last point on group shots is to let family members know they are going to be involved in these pictures ahead of the day. Honestly, if you take my word for anything in this book then make it this: the quicker you can get through these photos, the better for everyone!

## Couple's portraits

These usually come after your group photographs, when your photographer will take the two of you off for more private photos. Again, it may feel like the last thing you want to be doing, but these are the photos you will cherish forever. If you don't love having photographs taken, just pretend. You need to trust your suppliers – they will direct you and often the weirder you feel, the better the photo looks. Just remember you can't go back and do this again another day, so go with the flow.

## Under the veil

During photos, ask your partner and guests to put their hand under the veil when they pose, not over the top. This avoids the accidental tug on your head! Another tip to remember is that feet go under the dress. So, during group photos, lift your dress so that guests can get closer to you, then drop it on top of their shoes.

# MORE TO THINK ABOUT …

## Guestbook

This is likely to be out during your drinks reception and can act as a form of entertainment too. Personally, I say scrap the book – it will either be left untouched or full of penis drawings. Here are a few of my favourite alternative ideas:

**Audio guestbooks.** This one will always be a big fat win for me. What's better than hearing lots of lovely messages from your family and friends (and a few drunk Chinese takeaway orders at the end of the night)?

**Polaroid guestbook.** Your guests will love taking a photo to add to your book. They can leave a little message alongside it too. (Don't forget glue dots, pens and polaroid refills.)

**Jenga blocks.** A guestbook and a game for future – guests sign a Jenga block and add it to the tower.

**Sign something.** Are you travel lovers? Sign a globe. Music lovers? Sign a record. Do you love games? Sign a Monopoly board.

**Fingerprints.** Could be a little 2001, but you can create lovely art by getting your guests to leave a fingerprint on a picture.

**Photobooth.** A lot of photobooths also offer the guestbook as part of their package. Two copies of the photos are printed – one for the guests and one for the guestbook.

There are lots of quirky ideas for guestbooks so go for something that makes sense to you both as a couple. Don't be boring!

## Decor

The drinks reception is not a space that usually requires much decor, as such. However, it is good to consider how you can tie this area to the rest of the venue. Can you order additional bud vases to dot around on the tables? Is there a space where your group photos will take place and therefore require some styling?

I know you may be planning to be outside during this time, but be conscious that the weather is the only part you can't plan, so be prepared for Plan B.

# SIGNAGE

Personalized signage is always a winner. You could use any of the following for this part of the day:

**Order of the day** – this can be moved
from your ceremony.

**Table plan** – I recommend making this available during the drinks reception so guests know where they are seated and you avoid having a bottleneck when it's time to go in for dinner.

**Drinks sign** – to let guests know what
drinks are available.

**Food signs** – whether it's a menu for the canapés
or a pun on your graze board, I'm here for it.

**Card box sign** – a little 'thank you' is
always appreciated.

**Guestbook sign** – this could be a how-to guide,
or just a reminder to leave a message.

# Reception Timing Tips

Your drinks reception is when guests can mingle, chat with old friends, take photographs, have drinks and canapés, play lawn games, watch the magician, listen to music. Don't cut it too short because you're worried guests will be bored – this is probably the most enjoyable part of the day for them.

If you're just providing drinks, then I would allow one hour. This gives you plenty of time for photos but equally guests aren't going to get bored. If you are doing drinks and canapés, I'd say an hour and a half would be perfect. Everyone will be kept busy while you enjoy photos and time with your guests. If you have drinks, canapés and entertainment – for example, lawn games, magic or live music – I'd recommend between an hour and a half and two hours, depending on how much entertainment you're providing. Guests will have plenty to do and will be fed and watered – and they can't really ask for much more than that!

## Take some time together

Making some time to be together as a couple is one of the biggest tips I can give you, and your drinks reception is the perfect opportunity for it. The day will go so quickly – probably quicker than any other day in your life – so take the moments to really embrace it. Go for a little walk together, chat during your couples' photos, hide away for a few moments just to be together.

## Time to be seated

Guests will inevitably go to the toilet, put their coats away, grab drinks and chat to a few more people before their bums hit the seats, so it's good to allow at least fifteen minutes for this. Here are three reasons why you may need to extend this time:

1. You have a larger wedding with more than 100 guests. In this case, I recommend allowing between twenty and thirty minutes for everyone to be seated.

2. Your drinks reception space is quite far from the wedding breakfast space (for example, if you've had a marquee and there's a short walk to the dining area). Add the walk time to your timings.

3. You have an interactive table plan (see pages 117–18 for some examples). I would advise you allocate another fifteen minutes for guests to enjoy this.

This is time for the groomsmen to really shine. At the appropriate moment, they should make their rounds and let everyone know it's time to be seated – saying something along the lines of, 'We are now asking guests to take their seats for dinner ...'

CHAPTER 5

# The Wedding Breakfast

# It's food, glorious food ...

Let's call this the main event. I don't think it's the most important part of the day, but if you do this bit wrong it will forever be remembered! This is the moment to showcase to your guests what you're all about. Think of dinner parties you have thrown in the past – what went well and what are you known for? If you're all about the music and greetings, allow yourselves time for this. If the food does the talking, then sit down and shut up.

Once again, there are so many options available for you; so, when you're hunting for a venue, caterer or bar, remember to question the standard options they offer and push the boundaries and ideas a little – it's time to get creative.

# THE ENTRANCE

You can't possibly get married and then just walk into the room like nothing has happened, so you'll need an MC to help you and the wedding party make an entrance. You'll want to opt for someone loud, confident and important to you – it's a great role, and the right person will usually love it.

Firstly, nobody will hype you up like someone you love. Secondly, there will be photographs and it's always much nicer to have people you know in them. Finally, guests listen to one of their own a lot more than they listen to suppliers or venue staff. Cue your MC's first big role! They can announce lots of things, or just the essentials ...

## Essentials

- The couple's entrance into the wedding breakfast room

- Cake cutting (if you're having one)

## Optional extras

- Individual speeches

- Guests to be seated in the wedding breakfast room

- Guests to leave the wedding breakfast room

- First dance

They can take the opportunity to say a few words about you, but this is the main thing they will need to say on your arrival:

**Ladies and gentlemen, please be upstanding.**
[Pause for guests to stand.]

**Please put your hands together as
we welcome the new ...**

This part is up to you – are you Mr and Mrs Mitchell, The New Bride and Groom, Mr and Mr Davies, Your Beautiful Brides, Tom and Sally ...? You decide how you would like to be introduced!

## Music

Let's elevate that entrance a little bit more! The next thing we need to decide is what song you're walking in to. Is this essential? Nope. Should you do it anyway? Yes. Set the tone for the day and have a bit of fun! So, how to pick the song? Here are some ideas:

- **Something sentimental** – I went for a song that meant a lot to us: 'You've Got the Love' by Florence & the Machine; it was important to include that song somewhere in our day.

- **Ibiza hype** – if you want the energy and are going for a vibey wedding, how about something super-upbeat like 'Jubel'.

- **Rock 'n' rollers** – 'We Will Rock You' will get everyone banging the tables.

- **Traditional hits** – anything old school like 'This Will Be (An Everlasting Love)' will get the guests swaying like crazy.

Can you get your daytime musicians to play you in? Can you play an instrument and play yourself in? Can you come from different doors and do a *Dirty Dancing* lift? Can you piggyback? Do you want to come in and do a shot? Want to do a dinner dash? Am I making it clear that anything is possible ...?

Do you want your guests waving napkins? Do you want everybody to stay seated? Want them to create an arch that you run through? You do you, and use the opportunity to make this your wedding. Just make sure your MC knows so they can announce it properly.

### Let him lead

Gents, you may want to be polite and let your wife walk in front – but not today! You need to take the lead to allow room for the dress train. When you're making your entrance to the wedding breakfast, the dancefloor and so on, the groom should take the bride's hand and walk slightly ahead. (For same-sex couples who are both wearing dresses, whoever has the bigger train goes at the back!)

# SPEECHES

This is one of my favourite parts of a wedding day, but that's easy to say when you're not the person giving a speech! I can help you to get everything in place to make this perfect, and then it's over to the friends and family you're trusting to speak ...

### Who should speak?

Traditionally, speeches would be father of the bride, groom and best man – in that order. However, weddings have moved on a lot in the past century or two; so, honestly, pick whoever feels right for you.

I think it's good to aim for someone to speak on the couple's behalf (typically the groom), someone to speak for the bride (typically the father of the bride) and someone to speak for the groom (usually the best man's job), so I recommend you pick people who can do this – whether or not they're in the traditional roles.

## When should speeches be?

In wedding terms, this is like the chicken and the egg: there is no right and wrong. It just depends on the wedding you're having and when suits you best. I've made you a pros and cons list for each option:

### Pros before dinner

Nervous speakers? Get them out of the way so they can actually eat their food

The decor in the room still looks how you want it – with no red wine spills on the tablecloths and no gravy on shirts

### Cons before dinner

Guests may be starting to get hungry (you will definitely need canapés at the drinks reception)

It's not traditional

### Pros after dinner

Guests have had a few more drinks and will find everything funnier!

It's more traditional and may be when guests are expecting to hear speeches

### Cons after dinner

Guests may be restless and tired after eating their meal

It's hard to get everyone to sit back down after the meal

You should have a maximum of four speeches and allow forty-five minutes in total for them. If you're thinking of having more than four speeches, I highly recommend spreading them out and having some before and after the meal – or even putting some in the drinks reception or cocktail hour.

My strongest recommendation is that you do not put speeches in between courses! Not only is it super-inconvenient for your suppliers (the videographer will need to come in after each course, mic-up the speaker and set up cameras again), but it can also massively affect your food service. You can never guarantee how long speeches will take – it just doesn't work like that, even with timeslots – so food service can be delayed if they overrun, or you can end up with a gap in the service if they run quicker. Don't ruin your beef wellington! During the meal is also the only time guests get to fully relax, so let them enjoy their food and drink, chat to friends and enjoy this moment.

## What should be said?

The generalized guide I've provided gives you an idea of what should be included in speeches, based on the traditional roles already indicated. As I said, it's very uncommon for people to go super-traditional these days, though, so take this guide with a pinch of salt and feel free to amend where necessary.

## Father of the bride's speech

The main purpose of this speech is to speak about the bride, including her childhood, current life, achievements, stories and hopefully how proud the speaker is of them. This speech is sentimental and an opportunity for the father of the bride to talk about his daughter. Things I would include are:

- A welcome to guests and thanks for coming

- Stories about the bride – past and present

- A welcome to the groom's family

- How the FoB met the groom and stories about them

- Marital advice for the couple

- A final toast – to the bride and groom

## Groom's speech

This speech should mainly include the day's thank-yous, but it should also be about the bride – of course! I would include:

- An acknowledgement of the previous speech

- A welcome to everyone

- A toast to absent friends and family

## THANK-YOUS TO:

guests who have travelled

guests for coming

suppliers
(if appropriate)

groom's parents

bride's parents

bridesmaids

groomsmen
and best man

Stories about the bride
– how you met, qualities
you love, everything!

a final toast –
to the bride

## Best man's speech

Right, firstly, there is a fine line between funny and inappropriate.
Check who the audience are – how many grandparents and how
many children – and keep it clean enough not to offend. Secondly,
this speech should include:

- An acknowledgement of the previous speech

- Funny stories about the bride and groom and nice
comments about them as a couple (and how they met)

- A final toast – to the couple

Give your speakers a guide so they don't double up too much and thank the same people or toast the same absent friends and family. Get somebody neutral to have a look over all the speeches and check for duplication.

## Gifts

Don't hand out gifts during your speeches – it's not a quick process and is awkward for the people receiving them and the guests watching. Give them out in the morning or when the speeches are finished instead.

## Announcements

Have a think about how you want your speeches to start. Do you want your MC to announce each one, or should the first speaker just go straight into it? There isn't really a right or wrong with this; it's just good to know what's happening ahead of the day. My advice is to get your MC to announce the first speech, then each speaker announces the next.

**Top Tip:** Add a song clip to the start of each introduction – for example, 'Daddy Cool' before the FoB speech.

### No phones allowed

Maybe this is just a personal hate of mine, but please print the speeches! The phone-light glow can really ruin photographs, it's much harder for speakers to keep their place and it just doesn't look as good.

**Top Tip:** For very aesthetic weddings, print speech cards. These are plain backing cards containing your logo/date/name that hide the speech papers behind them.

### Microphones

This is a big one to think about – being unable to hear speeches is, to me, super-awkward and can really ruin that time in the day. I'd start by speaking to your venue about what is already available to use onsite. Most venues have some form of PA system and microphones for this – just check the quality.

If your venue has nothing available, consider hiring a microphone and speakers. You'll need them to play background music anyway, so it's money well spent. (Psst: you can often ask the band to set up a system, which can be a cheaper option.)

# BACKGROUND MUSIC

This is an absolute non-negotiable. There is nothing more awkward than a silent room. Hopefully your guests will all be chatting away and the vibe will be great, but let's help them out with a bit of background music, just in case.

You may be sick of me saying this, but it's my book, so I don't care: please personalize your day! Music is another free and easy way to go from a wedding to *your* wedding, so pick songs you both like. Maybe they are from the year you met, or your favourite singers, acoustic hits, pop, rock – anything! If you're really stuck and just going for romantic vibes, then acoustic covers on Spotify will sort you right out.

You can also opt for live music here. Again, it depends on the atmosphere you're going for but a piano will give a luxurious feel, singers will get the audience participating, sax will be a vibe – do what fits your wedding theme.

## Singing waiters

We can't talk about music and not cover this hugely popular option. Singing waiters are performers who act like waiting staff and then surprise guests by falling over and bursting into song. Love them or hate them, they are here to stay.

If you are looking to have singing waiters, your suppliers need to know! They will affect your timings, so your caterers will need to be able to accommodate this and you'll need to allow time in your timeline too. Your photographer and videographer should also be in place and ready to capture the surprise, so do consider them and any other suppliers you'll need to support your plan.

# Georgie's Timing Tips

The general rule of thumb is that each speech is ten minutes – yes, even if you tell them it's a strict five minutes. Guests will laugh, clap, cry and interrupt and this all adds time, so please don't underestimate how long it will take. If speeches are quicker than anticipated, then guests will have extra time for toilet breaks, pouring drinks and chatting. Alternatively, you're eating into your wedding breakfast time (excuse the pun).

Thirty minutes is the normal duration for speeches, but discuss this with your speakers and be conscious of whether they may take much longer. It's so important to get these timings as accurate as you can so you can plan the day well.

**Three speeches** – thirty minutes

**Four speeches** – forty-five minutes

**Five speeches** – one hour

**Six speeches** – just don't, at least not all at once

If you're splitting your speeches up, make sure you allow the necessary time in both slots.

Before we get onto the food, let's talk about the set-up of a wedding breakfast ...

# GUEST TABLES

This is hopefully on your list already, but do you have tables? Does the venue provide them? Do you need to hire your own? Are they rustic? Do they need cloths? Speak to your venue about what is available and what can fit in the space. Find out all your options, not just those for your guest numbers as they can change.

The pretty big question is whether you want round or long tables. I don't believe there is much difference in the ability for guests to chat to each other, so ignore that old wives' tale. It's more about the aesthetic of your wedding. Have a look at your mood board – have you subconsciously already chosen? Don't forget there are less used options too, like square tables (two trestles put together), U-shaped arrangements, one long table, oval tables or even a mix of all the above. My best tip for choosing is to think about the decor and the available space – it may also help to start plotting your table plan.

Maid of honour · Father of groom · Mother of bride · Groom · Bride · Father of bride · Mother of groom · Best man

## Top table

Where will you be seated? It's important to consider multiple things when deciding where you want to be seated:

**Windows.** Although they make a beautiful backdrop to the eye, windows can make photographs difficult. If it's sunny, it can also be quite blinding for guests, especially during the speeches, so where possible I would avoid having a window behind you.

**Being among all your guests.** I'd perhaps advise against sitting within an arrangement of long tables. Again, think ahead to your photographs: your background will be other people and it may be hard to get a lovely picture of you both, especially during speeches. I would also consider where the speakers will stand during speeches. You'll want them to be where they can easily see you both and also your guests.

**Busy areas.** I would try to avoid being anywhere where the foot traffic is high. You don't want to be sat by the bar, toilets or entrance, as your guests will be constantly walking around you and interrupting every mouthful you take.

**The shape of the top table.** Do you want to sit on a round table with your family and friends or do you want a traditional long table? Maybe you want to move away from the norm and opt for a sweetheart table instead ...

**Sweetheart table.** This is a table for just the two of you. It's a great opportunity to have some time alone together but is equally inviting for guests to come and say hi when the time is right.

Who should be on your top table? Traditional arrangements are less common these days, but the diagram on the opposite page gives you an idea of what the norm has generally been.

I would think about who you want to spend these two hours with. Do you want to stay traditional and sit with your families, or would you prefer to have friends with you? This has the potential to ruffle a few feathers, so it may be worth asking close family their opinion so you can understand if it would cause upset.

**Top Tip:** If your speakers aren't sitting on the top table, make sure you assign a space for them to stand during their speeches. This should be near you – to one side of the top table works well.

# CHAIRS

Surely you don't need to worry about chairs? Wrong! Does your venue offer chairs? What are the available chairs like? Are they ugly? Are they like conference chairs? If the aesthetic of your wedding is important, maybe you need to consider sourcing your own chairs. There are many options: ghost chairs, Chiavari chairs, Louis chairs, folding chairs, banquet chairs … the list goes on. Just to give you a very rough idea, chair hire starts from £5 per chair – so that's £500 for 100 guests. Make sure there's room in the budget.

Alternatively, you could cover the venue's chairs – but, honestly, this can look a bit outdated and 'hotel wedding 2003'. Other options include sashes, floral decorations or ribbons, so do think about all the ways you could spice them up.

### Matchmaker chair

Honour your matchmaker! Do you have a friend or family
member who was responsible for setting you up? Decorate
their wedding breakfast chair with a matchmaker sign,
flowers, balloons, a sash ... Anything at all – just let
everyone know they are all here because of them!

# WHAT GOES ON YOUR TABLES?

Now we have the basics of tables and chairs, let's work out what is
going on your tables. This is very dependent on the food you are
having – so you can work out a guide here, but also check with your
caterers. A sit-down three-course meal would usually have things like
knives, forks and spoons for each course, plus side plates, napkins,
condiments, glasses and so forth. Plus, we then add all your personal
additions – for example, wedding favours, name cards, charger
plates, table names, menus ... The list goes on. So it's very important to
think about how much space you need on your tables.

If you are having fewer than three courses, the amount of crockery
and cutlery will reduce. Equally, if you've opted for a family-style
meal, you'll need space for the sharing boards and bowls to go
down. This is all before you've even thought about table decor like
candles and florals, so just bear that in mind.

# DO I NEED TO ALLOCATE SEATS?

Simple answer – yes. The only time it's appropriate not have a table plan is when you're having street-food vans. Even then, however, it is important to remember:

- You need seating for every guest in case they all want to sit down to eat at the same time, but hay bales, sofas and picnic blankets can definitely work.

- You need space inside for every guest in case it rains.

- Some guests won't be able to sit together. When guests seat themselves, you will inevitably end up with random spare seats around the place and potentially some families having to separate.

For service, your caterers will need to know where specific guests are seated, especially those with dietary requirements. If you really want to avoid a table plan, you could allocate guests to specific tables but allow them to sit where they like at those tables.

# TABLE PLAN

This is the sign that shows guests where to head once they get into the wedding breakfast room. A table plan is a great opportunity to showcase some personality or your wedding theme, so utilize this. Interesting, interactive table plans are a great crowd pleaser and can create wonderful and funny pictures, or you might go for something traditional with your own twist. Here are ten table-plan ideas:

1. A classic sign with tables and names listed below.
2. Names listed alphabetically under table numbers.
3. Best buds – bud vases with guests' names and table numbers on them.

4. Shot wall – shots or small bottles of alcohol with guests' names and table numbers on them.

5. Love letters – little notes to each guest telling them what they mean to you that also include their table number.

6. Photo frames – this doesn't need to be one big board; you can have one frame per table and the names listed within them.

7. Photo wall – featuring photos of guests beneath their table name or number.

8. Library – each guest gets a book with their name and table number on.

9. Thrift-shop mugs – each guest has their own thrifted mug with their name and table number on.

10. Travel style – London Underground map, globes, maps with guests placed at certain locations.

You can use paper, a mirror, card, big boards, pumpkins, wine bottles, acrylic signs, wooden pallets – anything at all! Think of how you met, what you love, how you got engaged …

Remember that the table plan just needs to show guests which table they are on, not exactly where they're seated.

# NAME CARDS

These tell your guests exactly where they are seated when they reach their tables. If you can write a name on it, you can use it as a name card. Here are ten name-card ideas:

1.  **Folded cards** – the classic, with names printed on them.
2.  **Flat cards** – again, with names printed on them.
3.  **Polaroids** – a polaroid picture of each guest (don't forget to put names on the back for the caterers or whoever is setting this up for you!).
4.  **Drawings** – a drawing of each guest can be a favour and a name card.
5.  **Laser-cut names** – in wood or acrylic.
6.  **Leaves** – perhaps olive or eucalyptus leaves with guests' names written on them.
7.  **Favours** – add names to your favours: for example, on a packet of Smarties or seeds.
8.  **Coasters** – names written on acrylic, slate or wood coasters double up as favours to take home.
9.  **Drinks charms** – names on discs that sit on guests' glasses.
10. **Menus** – add guests' names to the top of their menus.

For the modern couple who met online, Tinder name cards are a great way to celebrate the app!

# MENUS

Menus aren't essential, but they are a nice touch. It's helpful for your guests to know what they're eating, as they will definitely have forgotten what was on your invites! You can give guests their own menus, but I recommend personalizing them with their meal choices. Alternatively, you can put a menu on each table. These can go in frames, laid flat on place settings, on the back of table numbers or as table talkers.

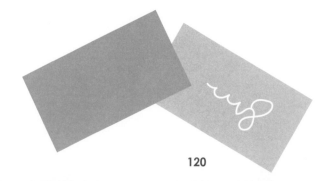

# TABLE NAMES AND NUMBERS

These are essential stationery items because they show guests which table is which and therefore where they are seated. Numbers are perfect for the classic, timeless wedding theme. However, I'm pro-personality and there are millions of ideas you can take inspiration from. If you use names, you can build a showcasing theme – using books, bottles of spirits, globes, records ... You get the point. For example:

- Countries you have visited

- Years of your relationship, shown in photos

- Ages with photos of you both

- Songs you love or which have meaning to you both

- Houses you've lived in

- Names of pets

- Book titles

- Film titles

- Cocktails or favourite drinks

- Trees, lakes, mountains, seasons

# DEALING WITH DROPOUTS

You hear about dropouts but never think it will happen to you.
It will, almost certainly! This might be a day guest who suddenly
can't get childcare despite having two years' notice, or the evening
guest who RSVPs yes but ghosts you anyway! The steps you're going
to take are:

- You have thirty minutes to be upset/annoyed/
  moan/strop – then get over it.

- Let your suppliers know – for example, your
  coordinator, caterer, venue.

- Remove the dropout's items from your boxes
  (if you've made up your table boxes, take their
  name cards out).

- Don't worry about any stationery you already have
  printed, such as your table plan; your guests only
  care about their own names.

It's also worth considering whether you could invite one of your
evening guests instead. Yes, it's a little awkward, but equally they
may be happy to step in and then you're not out of pocket!

# CELEBRATIONS ON YOUR DAY

If a guest is also celebrating something on your wedding day, it's nice to show you've thought about them. It's nice to be nice, so just find your level of sharing the spotlight! Here are a few ways to celebrate with them, in order of most to least attention:

- Celebrating a big anniversary – let them have the first dance.

- Birthday guest – let them cut the cake.

- During the speeches, sing to them (birthdays), mention them (anniversaries).

- Bring out a special cake during the dessert.

- Put a sign on their table – perhaps 'It's my birthday! When I drink, you all drink!'

- Pop a card or present on their place setting.

# FOOD

Let's start with why it's called the wedding breakfast. Ceremonies used to be a lot earlier in the day, so the name made a lot more sense. Now it's seen as the first meal you enjoy together married. This is potentially the most important food you will pick and it's the bit everyone is going to remember – whether for being good or bad. No pressure.

Remember that you need to keep your guests going all day, unless you want them leaving in search of food! So, when it comes to budgeting, ensure you have allowed for enough food (and if you need to, prioritize food over drink!). We all know from our teenage years that eating food helps us avoid getting too drunk too quickly, which is also something we want for our wedding guests. If you haven't given your guests canapés, I recommend getting them in and fed pretty quickly.

## Who can cater?

There are a variety of options, but start by thinking about who you are allowed to have. Look at what choices you have with the venue you have selected, as these will fall within three broad categories:

**In-house catering.** This is when the venue does all the catering themselves. They have a team of chefs and waiting staff and you will likely be restricted to using these. This is why it's so important to

know your options when you look for venues. If food is the most important aspect of the day to you, make sure those in-house caterers are perfect!

**Recommended suppliers.** Some venues don't have caterers onsite but do give you a select list of outside caterers to choose from.

**Outside catering.** Some venues, including marquees and teepees, allow you to have anyone you like! This is perfect for couples who really want a bespoke option. You select a caterer who will then be able to pop up a kitchen onsite and provide food as well as a team.

## Food service

Once you know who is allowed to cater your wedding, you can think about how the food will be served ...

**Traditional.** The traditional option is a three-course, sit down, formal meal. Love it or hate it, this is still very popular. You can also opt for a traditional format but add your own twist to the food options – it doesn't have to be chicken and potatoes if you don't want that. Think pie and mash, lasagne, trios of desserts. This is another time to add some personality to your day. Is there a food you both love? Is there a country you have visited whose food you love? Is there a family recipe?

**Family style.** Also known as sharing plates, family style is very popular! This is when you select food but it comes to the tables in big sharing bowls or platters. Usually mezze boards, carved meats, potatoes and salads, it is great for getting your guests to interact with each other and allows everyone to have exactly what they want. The only downside is the space you will definitely need on the tables, which means extravagant centrepieces may not work.

**Buffet.** This is when your food is served all together on a long table somewhere in the wedding breakfast room. If money is spent on the buffet table's styling and your caterers understand the brief, it could be beautiful.

**Street food.** Food vans are a great way to feed your guests and they don't just have to be for the evening. If you are going for festival, casual, big-family-gathering vibes, street food could be for you.

**Top Tip:** If any of your food will not be served to the tables, you must have your coordinator call guests up table by table to avoid big queues – nobody wants to stand in a queue at your wedding. You can also mix and match: you could have a sit-down meal with starter and mains, then a dessert buffet or an ice-cream van outside – anything goes.

### Do we need to feed suppliers?

You'll need to check your suppliers' contracts, but yes – unless you want them leaving midway through the day to get food and drinks, you'll need to provide something. Venues will usually give you a price for this, and it tends to be a main-course meal served during your wedding breakfast.

Generally, the suppliers you need to feed are those who have been there all day, such as your photographer, videographer and coordinator. It's always hugely appreciated by your suppliers – but also, a happy photographer means better photos!

# DRINKS

There is an expectation to provide some drinks during your wedding breakfast – typically wine, water and toast drinks. These are the basics you will need to cover to ensure your guests are well watered (and boozed!).

- Red or white wine will cover most guests, but do choose with your meal choices in mind. Generally speaking, red wine pairs well with red meats, whereas white pairs better with chicken and fish.

- Rosé lover? Include it! Summer wedding? Add more white wine! Winter wedding? Red's in!

- You can choose whether to add additional options such as buckets of beer or soft drinks. Be considerate of the guests who don't drink wine, and definitely don't forget about those who won't be drinking alcohol at all.

- Toast drinks are a great drink to have during the speeches, most popularly prosecco or champagne. However, feel free to get creative – shots, anyone?

- Will your caterers provide water? Do you have somewhere to refill jugs and bottles? Do you want sparking water?

## Quantities

Running out of drink is not fun for anybody, so it's essential to get it right.

**Toast drinks.** This is an easy one: you need to provide one per guest, and you get six glasses from a bottle of prosecco or champagne. Divide your number of guests by six to get your total, but over-order to allow for any damages, additional glasses and so on. (So, for example: 100 guests ÷ 6 = 16.7 bottles; extend that to 18–20 bottles for toasts.) Also get a non-alcoholic option such as no-secco or elderflower for toasts – it's nice to be thoughtful. Consider how many children and non-drinkers you are having, but allow for a few extras!

**Top Tip:** You can always add a touch of personality here too! What's your favourite drink? Or shot? Can you serve guests a Tequila Rose to toast instead?

**Wine for tables.** The rule of thumb is to provide half a bottle of wine per person, but it's good to look at your guest list. The benefit of a table plan is that you know who will be where. Do you have a whole table of children? Great, skip the wine! Table of wine lovers? Double up! It's OK to create a guide for your caterers to show where you need specific drinks.

**Water.** A litre jug of water will pour between four and six glasses. On a hot summer's day, you will go through a lot of water – so ensure these are being replaced or topped up throughout the wedding breakfast. If it's particularly hot, set up a hydration station too.

**Top Tip:** Buy your wine on sale or return – any that remains unopened can then be returned.

## Bar opening time

Speak with your bar company or venue to understand what options you have available and think about whether you want your bar to be open during the meal. There are pros and cons to this:

## Pros

Guests can have alternatives to wine (sometimes a coke or lemonade is required!)

It reduces the pressure to get the right quantity for the meal

## Cons

Guests can get drunk quicker

Guests leave the tables and gather by the bar

## What is corkage and should I use it?

Corkage is a fee that venues or bar companies use that allows you to bring your own alcohol for your guests to enjoy. The annoying thing about it is that you're paying on top of the alcohol you have already purchased, for it to be used at your own wedding. However, corkage does then usually include the storing, chilling and serving of your drinks – sometimes even the glassware and clearing of the bottles.

Corkage prices can vary from venue to venue. It's sometimes charged as a per-head or per-bottle rate, which can be anything between £5 and £25 per bottle! It can be beneficial if the available in-house drinks selection is more expensive than the price of your drinks plus corkage. It's also worth considering if you have a particular wine, champagne or beer that you want or that is special to you.

## Quick-fire drink questions

### What are toast drinks and do we need them?
Toast drinks are usually prosecco or champagne. These are poured ready for your guests to have while you're doing your speeches. You don't need specific toast drinks – guests can use the wine you have made available – but they are usually expected at a wedding.

### What if guests don't like wine?
You can pop beer buckets, wheelbarrows or tables around with beers, soft drinks, prosecco, ciders and so on – but check with your venue first.

### Is glassware important?
Yes! The glassware that you have during the wedding breakfast is part of the decor. There is no point having gorgeous flowers, crisp table linen and coloured napkins if you then have mismatched, short, thick glasses. If in doubt, ask to see the glassware. (And if it's bad, you can always hire your own.)

### Do all the wines go out on the table?
Typically, no. Check with whoever is doing your serving, but often they will put a bottle of red and white on each table and replace them as necessary throughout the meal.

### Can we have help-yourselves drinks?
I wouldn't advise this, but during the meal is the only time that it is *potentially* doable. However, I would consider whether you want your guests walking around during this time.

# Georgie's Timing Tips

So, how long will your wedding breakfast take? This is something you'll need to work out once you have checked with your caterers, but I can give you a guide in the meantime:

- Three-course sit-down meal for 100 guests – 2 hours' service

- Two-course sit-down meal for 100 guests – 1.5 hours' service

- One-course, sit-down meal for 100 guests – 1.25 hours' service

- Afternoon tea for 100 guests – 1.5 hours' service

- Self-service buffet for 100 guests – 1.5 hours' service

- Street-food vans for 100 guests – 2 hours' service

**Top Tip:** If you are having entertainment, such as an interactive band, singing waiters or games or quizzes, you'll need to add additional time for this – I recommend thirty minutes.

# THE TURNAROUND

When your food and speeches are finished, you'll need to let the guests know that's it's time to move. Typically, your wedding breakfast space will be being transformed into your evening space – so the quicker guests leave the room, the longer you get to party. If your evening space is separate, I still don't recommend going straight into the party. You need a bit of rest time and nobody wants to start dancing straight after a meal – think of it like swimming! Either way, there are a few ways to get your guests moving:

- Cut the cake – doing this at the end of the wedding breakfast makes a great transition point.

- Make an announcement – your MC can announce guests to the bar or reception rooms: 'Ladies and gentlemen, we are asking you to now make your way to the bar and lounges while we get this room ready for a party ...!'

- Serve tea and coffee – in a different area, of course.

This time of the day can be hit or miss and is often referred to as 'the lull'. My advice is don't fear the lull – embrace it. How do you want this time to feel?

**Chilled.** Some guests will want to relax before your evening gets going. They can get a cup of tea and a piece of cake and chat to more friends. Some guests might use this time to freshen up or check into their accommodation. You as the couple may like to enjoy spending some time catching up with people you haven't seen during the day.

**Pre-party.** If you're looking to start the party early, add some music and fun here. Get a saxophonist playing, get the bar open and ensure you both take some time to get involved.

**Cocktail hour.** Use this time to set the standards. Have signature cocktails handed out in boujee glassware for classy vibes. Nothing says 'cocktail hour' like proper drinks, so let them speak for you.

**Fun, fun, fun.** Beer pong, pool table, Ibiza anthems, photobooths, fire pits ... Give your guests loads to do and let them gravitate to what they find fun.

## How long does it take?

Whether you're opting for a break or need one while the room is turned around, you should allocate enough time but not too much – it's a fine line! Things to consider are:

- Is the room large enough to have your dancefloor and music set-up in place already? If so, do you want that to be an option? (Think marquees with multiple zones.)

- If your room is being turned around, ask your venue how long it will take for staff to move tables and tidy up and ask your band or DJ how long they need to set up.

- If you're opting to make this bit fun, be sure you're not packing so much in that it creeps into your evening time – just allow long enough to have a chill and mingle until your evening guests arrive.

The optimum time for a turnaround is between one to one and a half hours – anything longer and you'll need to start thinking about entertaining everybody again!

# EVENING GUESTS

Oh, the dreaded question of evening guests or not. This is a debate that has been running since the beginning of time – OK, probably not, but it feels like it. Here are the pros and cons you should think about:

## Pros

It's cheaper to have some guests attend in the evening rather than having everyone there all day

Evening guests bring an extra hit of energy

If they are people you'd like to see on a night out, they'll be fun!

You'll likely have a fuller dancefloor

## Cons

It creates a bit of hierarchy among invitees

You need to allow time to greet them

It's very much a personal choice, but if you are having evening guests you need to accommodate them well. Here are my tips to make your evening guests feel welcome:

- Their arrival time is crucial – ensure that the wedding breakfast has finished but that there's also time for your evening guests to get settled before the dancing starts.

- Ensure you say hello! It's important you're around to greet these guests.

- If budget allows, give them a drink.

- Give them all the information they need – such as taxi numbers, accommodation ideas and timings for the evening event.

The first tip here is the most important: make sure you set an appropriate arrival time. I've seen far too many weddings where evening guests were told to arrive too early and speeches weren't yet finished or desserts were still being eaten. This makes evening guests feel like a spare part.

Midway through your turnaround time is the best point for your evening guests to arrive. For example, if your cocktail hour starts at 7 p.m. and your first dance is at 8 p.m., inviting them for 7.30 p.m. is perfect. This gives you a buffer in case the wedding breakfast slightly overruns while also allowing newcomers to get a drink and mingle before they hit the dancefloor.

# TIMINGS

While your day will be unique to you, here's an idea of typical timings for you to work with:

**2.45 p.m.** drinks reception

**4.15 p.m.** guests to be seated

**4.30 p.m.** B&G entrance announced,
then straight into speeches (x3)

**5 p.m.** wedding breakfast

**7 p.m.** cake cutting, cocktail hour,
room turnaround

**7.30 p.m.** evening guests arrive

# CHAPTER 6

# The Evening Party

Why they're all
really here ...

The formalities are out of the way and once the first dance is done, you're free to party! This part of the day is about getting the key components in place so everyone has a great night. How do you want the evening to feel? Is it a big party? Is it wild? Is it tame and classy? Is it all about the music? Or the drink? Or just everyone chatting?

I would like to say here that this part of the book is mainly about how to create an epic party. However, if that's not for you, that's fine! I've seen many weddings that have ended the night with a quiz, or board games and background music. You know your guests a lot better than I do, so stick to your guns.

The next thing to consider is how you want the evening space to look. As your daytime space may well become your nighttime space, you should think about whether you want to change things like decor and furniture.

# CHANGE THE VIBE

## Furniture

You'll still need some tables there. Not all guests will want to dance all night, so having spaces for them to sit and chill is very important. Speak to your venue/caterer/coordinator about what you want and where. Equally, you don't want the room to be filled with tables – this is a party space, not a restaurant.

## Dancefloor

Is there a dancefloor already? Do you need to add one? They are definitely a great way of setting expectations for the night: here is a dancefloor – now dance! Dancefloors can be hired from external companies who can come and set up during the turnaround. You can also make it super-personalized by adding your wedding logo. Nothing says boujee like a personalized dancefloor!

**Top Tip:** A small dancefloor brings a great energy. If you have a big room, consider adding a dancefloor to keep it contained and busy.

## Lighting

What are your lighting options for the evening? We certainly don't want the 'big lights' on! That is a mood killer. There are many different lighting options if you're not happy with what's provided.

Uplighters (these can also be coloured – great in white rooms)

Fairy lights

Disco lights

Chandeliers

Light-up letters

Candles

Lighting is a part of weddings that often gets forgotten but is hugely important. You can set a tone very easily with the right lights. Candles and fairy lights – romantic. Uplighters and disco lights – party.

**Top Tip:** If you've had candles in the day, buy additional tealights and tapered candles so they can be refilled or changed for the evening.

## Clearing the room

What items do you want cleared? Get rid of the table plan, the charger plates, glassware, napkins and crockery. You want the space in the evening to be cleared but still pretty, so keep out the centrepieces, table names, candles and any decor you had. Ask for the decor from any tables that are being removed to be dotted around the place – for example, florals can go by the bar or next to the stage and so on.

## Additional extras

Do you have anything extra you want to put out? Dancefloor props, flip-flops, new signage? This is the perfect time to have these things put into place, ready for when guests re-enter. More on this later ...

The room is ready, the guests are ready, so let's get them in! This can be another announcement for your MC to make. Alternatively, if you open the doors people will soon wander in. Make sure there's background music playing to ease guests inside, as we don't want them partying just yet.

# CAKE CUTTING

You want your cake cutting to be just before or straight after something else. It's a little bit awkward, because your guests are essentially just watching you slice and smile for a photo, but here are some tips to make it better:

- Have someone do a countdown – a simple 'Ladies and gentlemen, let's give them a countdown – five, four, three, two, one ...' and then you cut.

- Make sure you know where you're cutting. Some cakes have false tiers and metal plates, so know your cake and work this out prior to cutting it in front of all your guests.

- Don't go too hard and fast – a nice slow cut will avoid the cake falling over.

- Feel free to have fun, feed each other a bit, have a kiss – make this part interesting for photos.

**Top Tip:** If you smash cake in someone's face (without pre-agreement), we will all hate you and your marriage could be over before the first dance.

There are four times that work for a cake cutting. We know it needs to be before or after something, so these are my clear favourites:

**After your entrance to the wedding breakfast.** Guests are all seated, your entrance is announced, a song plays, you walk in and straight to the cake, cut it and then sit down.

**After the speeches.** If your speeches are before the wedding breakfast, opt to cut the cake after this. The last person speaks, then announces your cake cutting.

**After the meal.** If you've had your speeches first, your cake cutting is a great way to end the meal and show guests that this part of the day is over. Guests will gather to watch, you cut the cake and they are announced out of the room.

**Before the first dance.** Two awkward traditions in a row! You can opt to have your cake moved onto the dancefloor during the turnaround. When guests come back into the room, they can gather around the cake, you cut, it gets moved to the side and you go straight into the first dance. Guests will then already be in the right spot to watch.

---

### DO NOT FORGET:

| | |
|---|---|
| Cake knife | Napkins |
| Cake stand | Takeaway boxes |
| Trays to serve cut cake | (if you want guests to leave with a piece) |

---

# THE FIRST DANCE

I know what you're thinking: the first dance is awkward; we don't know what we're doing; we'll just dance for ten seconds then bring everyone in ... But let me give you a fresh perspective. It is awkward, yes. But so is the whole day! By the time it's your first dance you will have already said vows in front of everyone, kissed in front of everyone, been announced into the room, given speeches – this is just one more thing, and by this point you'll be used to it. It's your final moment to really enjoy and embrace being centre of attention.

## We don't know what to do

Practise. I highly recommend having a few dancing lessons. They are fun to do, a nice date night for you both and will also fill you with confidence. You don't need to learn a routine if that's not for you, but just knowing how to hold each other and do a few spins will ease your concerns. If dance lessons aren't in the budget, that's fine – there's YouTube! Practise in your kitchen.

**Top Tip:** Record yourself practising in the kitchen. After your wedding, you can put your practice videos with your first-dance video to create a gorgeous memory.

## Dancing for ten seconds

Don't expect any good photos if you don't dance for long enough! It's hard to think about now, but you will probably really enjoy the moment, so don't rush it. You don't get it back. At the very least, it's good to keep going until after the first chorus. This gives your guests long enough to watch and your photography and videography team to capture the dance. I recommend listening to your song and finding the natural 'drop', when it really comes in. Invite guests to join in at this point.

**Top Tip:** If you're really looking for something extra, add confetti canons (if they're allowed) – one to go off when it's just the two of you dancing and one that drops when your guests join you.

## What song to pick

Sentimental wins here – this song should give you the serious feels. It doesn't need to be a crowd pleaser, but it should be one you can dance to. There are acoustic versions of most songs, which is a great way to make pop songs more 'weddingy'. Alternatively, if you're having a band, you can ask them to play your chosen song slower. If you have no idea when it comes to picking a song, there are some tips to get you thinking on the next page. When in doubt, just pick something you love!

Songs from the year you met

Songs from your favourite film

Theme songs from your favourite TV shows

Lyrics are key – find a song that
says something meaningful

## The next song

Now, this is important. The one time you can absolutely guarantee a full dancefloor is just after your first dance – so we have to keep everyone there! What song will get you dancing?

# Georgie's Timing Tips

Your first dance is what gets the party started — I can say from experience that etiquette dictates nobody dances until you have. It's common practice to time your first dance for after the evening guests have arrived so they can be involved in this part of your day. There are a few other things to think about too:

- What time does your venue close?

- Can you extend that time with a late licence?

- What atmosphere do you want? (If you're in a marquee in summer, it doesn't get dark until 9.30 p.m., so I would advise against a 6 p.m. first dance as dancing in the daylight is a bit weird.

- How long are your band or DJ performing for?

- How long do you want for dancing overall?

To give you the timing guide you're dying for:

- **7 p.m.** too early (unless you've got an 11 p.m. finish)

- **7.30 p.m.** only OK in winter

- **8 p.m.** perfect

- **8.30 p.m.** fine

- **9 p.m.** pushing it, but if you've had a good cocktail hour then it's acceptable

- **10 p.m.** don't bother, unless you have a later finish time than midnight, you're having a destination wedding or you want something a little different

# MUSIC

Let's go out on a limb and say this is the hardest thing to nail, but here are your options:

- Full band

- DJ

- DJ and live instrument (for example, sax)

- Live musician (for example, pianist, singer)

- Speaker system

All of these can work; it just depends on your budget, vibe and guests. There is no point spending the money on a full band if you think your guests won't be up for dancing. Equally, a playlist won't give you the same interaction as a DJ will. So, think about your crowd and make your choice wisely.

## Music type

Now, it's your day. However, if you are both drum-and-bass enthusiasts, maybe don't fill the entire evening with your music taste. You still want your guests to enjoy themselves, presumably ... A great way to get a feel for what your guests want is to ask, 'What song will get you dancing?' on your RSVP. This is super-easy on a wedding website and will help you to create your wedding playlist. It's nice to play a mix of classics – think Shania, ABBA and Spice Girls – but then throw in a mix of your favourites that are potentially more modern.

## Playlists

Create a playlist, even if it's just a guide for your band or DJ. It's good for them to know what kind of music you like and – even more important – what you don't like! The last thing you need to play after your first dance is a song that makes you think of your ex. So make them a list of any vetoed songs. Equally important is making sure the setlist doesn't feel like something from a school disco.

## Times for music

Often bands will break their performance down into three forty-minute sets or two one-hour sets. There are arguments for both – some say an hour gives them chance to get going, while others argue it's better to spread the performance out as much as possible. It's also important to look at your evening timings and consider things such as when you're required to stop the music. If you've opted for an earlier first dance time, it could look like this:

**7 p.m.** first dance and first band set (forty minutes)

**8.20 p.m.** second band set (forty minutes)

**9 p.m.** break and evening food

**10 p.m.** third band set (forty minutes)

**10.45 p.m.** DJ

This way allows you to spread out the dancing. However, you may not have time to fit in three sets if you've opted for a later first dance, so just play around with your timeline.

**7 p.m.** finish wedding breakfast – turnaround

**8 p.m.** first dance and first band set (one hour)

**9 p.m.** break and evening food

**10 p.m.** second band set (one hour)

**11 p.m.** DJ

**Top Tip:** Create a games table for guests to help themselves to – they may want to chill and play, or they might turn them into drinking games. Either works!

## Keeping that dancefloor full

Here's your shopping list for keeping the dancefloor energy going. But my biggest tip is that you make sure you both spend time on that dancefloor! Guests will naturally gravitate to where you are, and you set the tone for the day, so show them what to do and bust some shapes ... Or at least try.

- Dancefloor props (blow-up guitars, microphones, saxophones).

- Glow sticks – anything guests can sing into and wave around their heads.

- A smaller dancefloor – guests like to dance near each other!

- Sunglasses – they give you a new persona ... One who likes to dance!

# EVENING FOOD

A question that often arises is whether it's necessary to provide evening food. An easy rule to follow is that if your guests have more than four hours of party left, you need to feed them again. So, for example, if you finished your wedding breakfast at 7.30 p.m. and the night ends at 12 a.m., you need food.

There are three ways to provide your evening food:

**Food trucks.** This will be the most expensive option, but it's arguably the most fun and interactive. Anything from pizzas to tacos, to pasta, to sushi – this is an easy way to add some personality to the day.

**Buffet.** Don't fear the word buffet – it doesn't need to be beige! Think more like graze boards, food stations, cheese and crackers or a mashed-potato bar ... (I know that's beige, but it's worth it.)

**Tray service.** Most venues will offer this as standard. Think about options such as bacon baps, fish-and-chip cones and sliders.

**Top Tip:** Every part of the day has personalization potential – add your logo to parchment paper for use with your evening food.

## How many people should I feed?

I've made a rule for this too! When in doubt, more is better than less, but you certainly don't need to feed 100 per cent of your guests. Do have boxes or bags so people can take food home with them, though – everybody loves cold pizza ... A guide for the maths is to assume you're feeding 70 per cent of your daytime guests and 80 per cent of your evening guests. So, for example ...

- If you have sixty day guests and thirty evening guests, you're feeding sixty-six guests

- If there are a hundred day guests and a hundred evening guests, you're feeding a hundred and fifty people.

# AN IRISH GOODBYE

This is the term used for someone who leaves a gathering or party without saying goodbye. In normal circumstances, this is incredibly rude. However, I am all for it at weddings. Let's set the scene: you're mid-'R.E.S.P.E.C.T.' on the dancefloor, hands in the air, heart-shaped flashing sunglasses on, surrounded by your friends, when twenty of your aunts and uncles drag you away to say goodbye. Here's a poem you can display to politely tell everyone to let you rave on:

If you need to leave our wedding
but the timing's not quite right,

Please don't interrupt the dancing –
we'll be partying all night.

Irish goodbyes are all the rage,
so don't feel bad or rude,

Just know we've loved having you
and will catch up very soon.

You can pop this in the toilets, on your newspapers, on your website – or (just to make sure everyone sees it) all of the above!

CHAPTER 7

# Happy Wedding Day!

# Set your mood for the day

It's officially the day you've been waiting for. You will be terrified, excited, feel sick, feel calm ... Just roll with these emotions. Something nobody will warn you about is that you'll also be bored! There is so much hype surrounding the day that you'll be very ready for it. But then the morning comes and you've got to wait around until 1 p.m. till it all gets going.

Starting the day right is crucial for your mood on the wedding day. Think back to times when you've had a stressful morning and how it's affected the rest of the day. These are my tips for having a stress-free and – dare I say it – fun wedding morning ...

# THE NIGHT BEFORE

To ensure your morning goes off without a hitch, there are a few things you need to do the night before. Here's your to-do list:

**Put a notebook by your bed.** When you're trying to sleep and little things pop into your head, just jot them down. I remember writing things like, 'Remind Dan to pick up Nan.'

**Steam the dresses.** This is definitely a night-before job – you really don't want to be steaming dresses on your wedding morning.

**Clean your engagement ring.** If you haven't had this done professionally before now, the night before is a good opportunity to get it sparkling.

**Have a bath.** A little de-stress works wonders the night before your wedding. Maybe treat yourself to some nice bubbles – but do not use any products you haven't used before.

**Have a drink.** It's OK to need to chill yourself out a bit, but don't get too drunk! A wedding-morning hangover is not a vibe.

**Tidy the getting-ready room.** If you're getting ready where you're staying, make sure it's tidy and ready for the morning. Get rid of any clutter or items you don't want in photographs.

**Flat-lay items.** Get anything you want for this photograph set out – for example, perfume, invitations, jewellery and shoes.

**Set out gifts.** If you have gifts for your bridesmaids, get them all out and ready.

**Remove labels and tags.** The little labels in the side of your dress, the hanger straps and most definitely the labels on the bottom of your shoes!

**Do your skincare.** Give yourself a little extra time to do your skincare the night before – again, don't use anything new.

**Wash your hair.** It's good to check with your hair stylist when you need to wash your hair. Sometimes it's good to have 'dirty' hair, but usually they will say to wash it the day before.

**Pack your wedding handbag.** This always gets forgotten and brides end up throwing in whatever they find in the morning. Get it ready the night before (lipstick, perfume, money, mini-emergency kit ...).

**Take off hairbands, socks and bra.** Let's not have any red marks and lines!

**Record yourself a message.** It's always nice to relive these memories, so record or write a little message to your future self.

**Stick on a TV show.** Nothing calms me down more than *Friends* playing as I go to sleep, so stick on a show and just shut your eyes.

**Accept the nerves and excitement.** Don't try to ignore the feelings – embrace them, enjoy them and most importantly sleep through them!

**Top Tip:** For cleaning your engagement ring, a dazzle stick works wonders – but if you don't have one, just use some very warm water and washing-up liquid. Leave it to soak for twenty minutes before gently brushing with a soft toothbrush, then rinse off and dry.

My final note on the night before is to think about what you're going to be doing. Do you want to go out for a meal? Do you want to be chilling at home? With friends and family or even alone? It's good to make a plan for the evening so you can be in charge of what is happening. Go to bed at a reasonable time and enjoy your last night as a singleton.

Now on to the morning ...

# BRIDESMAIDS

I recommend giving your bridesmaids a few jobs, such as:

- **Music master** – put someone in charge of keeping the vibe going and providing a speaker ...

- **Food chief** – someone needs to have food organized and feed you!

- **The cleaner** – that room needs to be tidy for photos, so someone should be keeping it that way!

This is your time to let them shine! Let them get you drinks and make sure you're fed and watered, happy and ready to go.

# MORNING TIMELINE

There is a lot to be done in a short amount of time, so planning your morning timeline is crucial. Between hair and makeup for multiple people, a group of women trying to get dressed and registrar interviews, it's tight. So, work with your hair and makeup artists and make a plan to stick to.

The perfect timings for an onsite wedding are:

- **Bridesmaids** – totally ready and in dresses one hour before the ceremony.

- **Bride** – dress starts to go on one hour before the ceremony.

- **First looks** – around thirty to forty-five minutes before the ceremony (depending on how many you have).

- **Registrar interview** – if you're having one, it will be fifteen minutes before the ceremony.

So the timeline for the most popular ceremony time of 2 p.m. is:

- **12.45 p.m.** bridal party gets dressed, ready for 1 p.m.

- **1 p.m.** bride's dress on

- **1.20 p.m.** first looks with bridesmaids and FoB

- **1.40 p.m.** photos, chill, nervous wee

- **1.45 p.m.** interview with registrar

- **2 p.m.** ceremony

Don't forget to allow travel time if you are getting married offsite.

# WHAT TO WEAR?

If your ceremony is at 2 p.m. and you wake at 7 a.m., that's over a third of your wedding day you won't spend in your dress. So, while I highly recommend getting a wedding dress you love, the getting-ready outfit will actually be featured a lot. There are a few things to consider:

**Does it look good?** Whether you go for the classic white PJs with feather sleeves, have a personalized dressing gown or go for a tracksuit, make sure you love the look, as it will be in a lot of photographs.

**Is it comfortable?** This is an obvious one, but you'll want to feel comfortable – maybe even cosy – on your wedding morning, so be conscious of this.

**Does it have easy access?** No, not that! When you've had your hair and makeup done, the last thing you'll want is to be pulling that top over your head – so think of your quick escape. Button-up PJs are a great option for this reason.

**Is there a theme?** If your wedding is a neutral delight with monochrome accents throughout, your photo album is going to be very upsetting if you're then featured in mismatched rainbow PJs. Just be conscious of how all the photographs will look together.

**Top Tip:** In case you hadn't thought about this ... You don't want to sleep in this outfit the night before! It is purely aesthetic, so think of it as your getting-ready outfit, not your nightwear. Make sure it is clean, ironed and ready to go. You don't even have to put it on until your photographer and videographer arrive.

While we're on the subject of what to wear, let's think about bras, socks and pants. Do you need to wear a bra during the morning? Have you gone for a strapless dress and therefore bra lines are a no-no? As a fuller-busted lady myself, there was absolutely no way I was going to be without something under my PJs, so I opted for a sports bra to hold them in place for the getting-ready pictures.

What underwear do you need for your dress? Make sure this is all ready to go – but I'd recommend putting it on when you put the dress on, so make sure you've got some getting-ready undies. If you're in white PJs, your comfy black granny pants probably won't look great, so go for something inconspicuous.

And if I see you wearing socks on the morning of your wedding, I'm personally going to come there and shout at you! You don't need them on, and they'll just create lines on your legs.

# BLOW ME!

**B**ouquets out of water. Trust me, you do not want your bouquet leaving a nice wet patch on your vagina – and that's what will happen if you leave your bouquet standing in water till the last minute! Most bouquets are delivered in a little vase of water. One hour before your ceremony, remove the bouquet from the vase, wrap a towel around the stems and pat them dry. Empty the water from the vase and put the bouquet back inside so it stands upright. Bridesmaids, this applies to you too. You need to do this in plenty of time to allow the stems to fully dry.

**L**ady-garden low. Speaking of your bouquet, you need to hold it low! Think pubes not boobs, hips not tits, flower to flower ... However you choose to remember it, keep it low! Find out from your florist which way round it goes (often the pins go at the back) and practise holding it low enough. It should be slightly lower than what feels comfortable, with your hands placed gently over one another to hold it – but if you need to hold someone's hand or your dress, just keep it nice and low with the other hand.

**O**ne hour. You should get dressed one hour before you need to leave for your ceremony or registrar interview. This hour passes at a different speed – much quicker than a normal hour – and you won't believe it until it's too late, so hear my warning. One hour before means it's time to go to the toilet, put the right underwear on, get your shoes, jewellery and perfume ready, then put that dress on!

**W**rists and ankles. Be conscious of anything that can leave marks on your skin. As discussed, hairbands on wrists and sock lines are the obvious ones, but also consider bra straps, jewellery and tight clothing. You don't want any visible marks or indentations on your skin when you walk down the aisle – so strip it all off the night before!

**M**ove your engagement ring. You'll decide when you pick your wedding bands whether yours is going to sit under or on top of the engagement ring. The large majority go under it, closer to the heart – and if this is the case for you, you'll need to move that engagement ring. Pop it onto your other hand, give it to a family member or put it in a bag, but keep it safe till after the ceremony.

**E**nergy. The tone of the day is seriously set by you, and this starts the minute you wake up! Get the music playing, get the buck's fizz flowing and enjoy that morning. It's a long part of the day, so don't spend it bored! Fill it with fun and laughter – *you are the fucking vibe!*

**Top Tip:** Anybody (including you!) who is going to touch the dress must wash their hands!

# TIDY SPACE

You will be having photos taken while you're getting ready, so be conscious of the space you are in. If the room is a mess, this will be obvious in the photos.

It'll be difficult to keep the whole room clean and tidy while multiple women are getting ready, but make sure there is a side of the room that's kept clear. Where will you be doing your first looks? Where will you be putting your dress on? These areas need to be looking good.

Remember to assign one bridesmaid the job of keeping things tidy!

# GETTING YOU DRESSED

Who do you want to help you put your dress on? Your morning may have been filled with noise, hustle and bustle, so you may want to take a few quieter minutes with just one person. Typically, this will be a mother, sister or bridesmaid, but some brides opt to go it alone or with their coordinator.

## Tips for dressing

- Ensure you have a private space to put your dress on (or just kick everyone out while you do it).

- Make sure you've removed any tags from your dress.

- Put your dress on the floor and step into it (this is best for most dresses).

- Spend time making sure you are comfortable (get those boobs in the right place).

- Get yourself decent and then invite the photographer or videographers back into the room – leave zips or buttons undone until they are there to capture that part.

- Add shoes, jewellery and perfume after your dress is on.

## Bridal prep photo ideas

- Putting in earrings

- Looking down and playing with the bouquet

- Playing with your engagement ring

- Looking at or touching your dress

- Spraying perfume

**Top Tip:** Brides, if you ever feel like you don't know what to do with your hands, pretend you're holding a small sweet such as a Skittle and play with it between your index finger and thumb. This looks very delicate in photographs – especially the ones during bridal prep.

### Bustling your dress

Bustling your dress is when you clip or tie it up, which shortens your train. Your seamstress will discuss this with you, but I highly recommend having a bustle as you won't know how you'll feel on your wedding day. There's nothing worse than just wanting to party and having your train get in the way.

**Top Tip:** Ask your bridesmaids to record how the dress is bustled at the shop. On the day, when everyone's drunk, it can be almost impossible to remember what was said!

# THE BOYS

Getting-ready tips for the men are a little less intense. Write a checklist in advance for what needs to be brought on the morning – I cannot tell you how many times shirts, trousers and rings are forgotten! Make sure everything is steamed and ironed ahead of the day too.

I usually advise that you have the men onsite (where the ceremony is happening) about ninety minutes before the ceremony. Guests will start to arrive around an hour before, so someone must be there to meet and greet. Having the men there at least one hour before gives them a chance to settle nerves, have a beer and chill.

### Gents' prep photo ideas

Have you arranged for photos of the men getting ready? A good tip is to ensure the groom and groomsmen are all dressed and set apart from their ties, cufflinks and jackets. This means the photographer can get the getting-ready photos but without those tighty-whities that no one wants to see. Here are some photo ideas for the men:

- Hands in the pockets
- Straightening tie/bow tie
- Putting shoes on
- Leaning against the wall
- Putting jacket on

# FIRST LOOKS

Ignore the couple's first look for now and let's think about the morning first looks with your parents and bridal party. Who do you want to set these up with? Remember, there will be a moment where these people see you for the first time, so you may as well capture it. I recommend starting with the bridal party. Ensure you are standing somewhere looking great (train in place, veil perfect) and get someone to bring the bridal party in with their eyes closed: three, two, one, open! This gives a great reaction photo.

Next up is often the father of the bride (or whoever is walking you down the aisle). They can do something similar to the bridal-party idea above, or just walk into the room and see you.

## Couple's first look

This is a big question to consider: do you want to do a first look together before your ceremony?

### Pros

A pre-ceremony first look is great for couples who are nervous – it can help ease the anxiety that comes with walking down the aisle

If you're having a late ceremony, it gives you the opportunity for couples' portraits in daylight (and means you don't miss the drinks reception!)

It's more intimate – it's lovely to have some time together before the madness of the day starts

### Cons

You don't get the 'end of the aisle' moment – for some couples this matters and for others not so much, so it's totally up to you!

If you do choose to do this, speak to your photographer about where and how. You'll need to avoid any guests arriving but also ensure it's a lovely spot. And don't worry – you can still do a traditional entrance and walk down the aisle after a first look!

**Top Tip:** If you allow enough time for a first look, you can go offsite to do it – think the local beach, a bar or a hilltop!

# RAPID-FIRE TOP TIPS

Here are some ideas for fun things to include in your morning ...

**Make your wedding hangers cute.** You can make lovely little labels with your printer at home. A little bit of ribbon and a name printed onto nice paper – done!

**Use grips to secure your veil.** Sometimes hairdressers will say, 'It's fine, I've backcombed it!' or, 'You'll be removing it later.' This is where you insist. I've often ended up putting a grip in to secure a bride's veil myself, because they can get caught on the carpet or pulled out when somebody gives the bride a hug just before the ceremony. So stand your ground and request those grips!

**Wait to give gifts or read letters.** Save this until your photographer and videographer arrive – these are moments you will want to capture.

**Use a mannequin for your wedding dress.** It looks better in photos and holds your dress really well.

**Use cotton buds (Q-tips) to stop your tears.** I don't recommend this throughout the day, but they're certainly good during the emotional morning. Just place one gently in the inner corner of your eye to stop the tears ruining your fresh makeup.

# PRACTICE

Most ceremonies don't include practice time, so make sure your bridesmaids have a quick pep talk in the morning or the night before, so they understand what they are doing. Do they have reserved seats? Are they walking in together? Do they sit, stand, kneel?

Have them spend five minutes practising walking in with nice gaps in between them. Make sure they know how to hold their bouquets and roughly where they will be sitting. Confident bridesmaids are happy bridesmaids!

Each bridesmaid will enter, stop at the start of the aisle (this is their chance to get their latest profile picture), smile and walk – slowly. The words I whisper to bridesmaids before they start that walk are:

**Lady garden** (lower that bouquet)

**Tits and teeth** (shoulders back, smile)

**Slow** (don't run down that aisle)